# THE MINISTER'S HANDBOOK

# Other Books:

**Preaching that Empowers God's People**:
*Expository Preaching in the 21<sup>st</sup> Century*

**Conducting Church Audits**: *A Guide for Internal Auditors*

**A Pastor's Introduction to Church Administration:**
*Administering the 21<sup>st</sup> Century Church Effectively*

# REVISED EDITION

# THE MINISTER'S HANDBOOK:
## *A Guide for Leadership*

JEREMY W. ODOM

Big O Publishing Group

©2016

ISBN: 978-0-9970-9563-0

Published by Big O Publishing Group
Natchitoches, Louisiana

The author has worked to ensure that all information in this book is accurate as of the time of publication. As research and practice advance, however, standards may change. For this reason it is recommended that readers evaluate the applicability of any recommendations in light of particular situations and changing standards.

Big O Publishing Group has made every effort to tract the ownership of all quotes. In the event of a question arising from the use of a quote, we regret any error made and will be pleased to make the necessary correction in future printings and editions of this book.

Library of Congress Control Number 2016905818

Printed in the United States of America

This book is dedicated to the memory of my beloved Father in the Gospel Ministry Rev. Joseph D. Dupree, D.Th. who inspired me to pursue my aspirations as an author.

This book is also dedicated to the Pastors and ministers who make up the Louisiana Ministerial Association, Inc. who have permitted me the blessed privilege to lead them to higher heights in ministry.

I also dedicate this book to my Pastor Rev. Mitchell C. Herndon, Sr., D.Div. who has been a huge supporter of my ministry for the past six years. Your contributions to my success are surely noted.

# Contents

# Foreword

Rev. Jeremy W. Odom has compiled some useful information pertaining to ministerial etiquette. The material is formatted in such a fashion that it lends itself quite easily to class instruction and/or to informal workshop initiatives. I especially recommend the part on leadership for beginning ministers and as a gentle reminder to seasoned pastors. This compilation drives home the thought that the main objective is not to place emphasis on oneself but upon God.

Herbert V. Baptiste, Sr., D.Min.
Former Director
United Theological Seminary & Bible College
Natchitoches, Louisiana

# Preface

This book was written as a tool to aid both young and seasoned ministers in the finer points of the Gospel Ministry.

This book carries one main theme for the young preacher which is the course moving from being a good follower to leadership. Senior pastors will find this book to be a invaluable resource when developing the ministerial training program for their young associates.

Having presided over the Louisiana Ministerial Association for over 8 years now, I can share with you the dangers of the minister's lack of pulpit etiquette.

This handbook was written to help the minister accomplish the following tasks:
- ➤ Understand the Call to Minister
- ➤ Protect & Promote your Pastor
- ➤ Young Minister Pitfalls to Avoid
- ➤ Finding Balance in Your Ministry
- ➤ Identify the different leadership styles

The goal is for the reader to develop an approach to ministry with a spirit of excellence. The reader will find several tools to better prepare themselves for the vocation in which they were called encased in these two covers.

I would strongly encourage the reader to take some time to complete a Spiritual Gifts Inventory so that you can have a better knowledge of your specific calling. There are several of these available online to accomplish this task.

I would also caution the Associate Minister to remain faithful to your calling, obedient to your pastor and most importantly diligent in your prayer life. Even when I began pastoring, I always gave reverence to my Pastor knowing that God will reward us for our obedience and faithfulness.

Each of us has a unique ministry that we have been called to serve. In my study, I have compiled a wealth of information that will help us to grow as ministers by teaching us to cope with our pastor, our calling and other ministers.

I would encourage you to include the books listed in the bibliography into your personal libraries for further in depth discussion into the subject materials which are presented herein.

JEREMY W. ODOM, D.DIV.

# Introduction

"The Minister's Handbook" is a most useful book for anyone currently in the pastorate or who is contemplating becoming a pastor. For that matter, it is a useful book for the layperson, particularly those who hold an office in the congregation, such as elder or deacon, and who have frequent contact with the pastor or pastors of the church.

Dr. Jeremy Odom, the author, has been a pastor for a number of years and currently serves as the General President of the Louisiana Ministerial Association. He presents his accumulated experience and wisdom in a way that is well-organized and easy to understand. In the first chapter of the book he gives some general practical advice to ministers, including on such diverse issues as knowing your gifts and talents, knowing your limitations, knowing how to handle conflict, managing on-the-job stress, and knowing how to plan and communicate.

In the second chapter, "Leadership Through Excellence," Odom discusses different types of leadership, such as transactional leadership, transformational leadership, charismatic leadership, and servant leadership. The third chapter ("The Pastor") speaks to the characteristics of a pastor as well as his identity and authority.

Finally, the last chapter, "The Pastorate," provides a great deal of practical advice to pastors and prospective pastors. Along with advice to new pastors, Odom discusses the three stages of a pastorate (getting underway, maturing relationships, ending positively) and looks at practical issues such as understanding the call (Odom provides a checklist of matters that should be clarified when a new pastor is called), do's and don'ts on changing the status quo, and implementing change.

# About the Author

**Dr. Jeremy W. Odom** is the General President of the Louisiana Ministerial Association, Inc. He is a Professor of Christian Ministry at the Southern Christian Bible College and Seminary where he also serves as Dean. He also serves as the Chairman of the Board of Trustees for the National Pastors and Ministers Conference.

Dr. Odom acknowledges being called into the Gospel Ministry at the tender age of six while attending Damascus Missionary Baptist Church of Lena, Louisiana under the leadership of Rev. William Batts. However, Dr. Odom did not preach his Apprenticeship Sermon until the age of fifteen at the First Baptist Church Amulet of Natchitoches under the guidance of Rev. Dr. Joseph D. Dupree.

Dr. Odom has served in the Gospel Ministry in many various positions. He has served as a Youth Pastor, Assistant Pastor, Senior Evangelist, Elder, Prison Chaplain and eventually Senior Pastor. His ministry has been heard all across America and in combat areas of Iraq.

Dr. Odom is the author of several books that are currently being utilized by seminaries, Bible students, preachers, teachers and scholars worldwide.

Dr. Odom has earned countless awards, including those from President of the United States, Department of the Army, Mayor of Natchitoches and Who's Who? He is a member of the Prince Hall Free & Accepted Masons hailing from Dawn of Light Lodge #22 in Natchitoches, LA. In 2012, he was awarded the Honorary Doctorate of Divinity from the American Bible University.

A native of Natchitoches, Louisiana, Dr. Odom has been licensed to preach since 2002 and an ordained minister since 2008. He currently serves as an Associate Minister of the First Baptist Church-North of Natchitoches, LA under the divine leadership of Dr. Mitchell C. Herndon, Sr.

*"Do all the good you can, by all the means you can, in all the ways you can, in all the places you can, at all the times you can, to all the people you can, as long as you ever can"*
**That is Greatness**

- JOHN WESLEY

# Chapter 1 The Minister & His Ministry

## The Minister of God

You have been given the greatest ministry in the entire world, that of ministering to people and reconciling them to the Lord and Majesty of the universe, God Himself. For this reason, you must understand and be fully committed to the great ministry He has given you.

### 1. You are chosen by God Himself.

It is God the Father - The only living and true God, the Sovereign Lord and Majesty of the universe - who has called and chosen you to be a minister. You have been given the highest privilege in the entire world: you have been called and chosen to be a minister by the Lord GOD Himself.

*Isaiah 43:10; Isaiah 44:6, 8; Jeremiah 1:5-7*

### 2. You are chosen by Jesus Christ.

It is the Son of the living God, Christ Jesus, who has called and chosen you to be a minister. He has chosen you to go and bear fruit among men. You are the most privileged person in the entire world: you have been chosen to be a minister - chosen by the Son of God Himself.

*Acts 20:28; John 15:16; 1 Timothy 1:12*

### 3. You are chosen by the Holy Spirit of God.

It is the Holy Spirit of God who has called you to be a minister. He has chosen you so that He can live within you - chosen you to be His instrument, His channel, His person through whom He can live and work upon earth.

- *The Holy Spirit wants to use your body and your life to show how a person is to live upon earth.*
- *The Holy Spirit wants to conform you to the image*

1

*of Christ - to make you an example for the world, an*
*example of how God wants people to live: in all godli-*
*ness and righteousness.*
• *The Holy Spirit wants to use you to preach and*
*teach the glorious gospel of Jesus Christ.*

You have been given the most glorious privilege in the entire world. You have been called and chosen by the Holy
Spirit of God: you have been called to live just like Christ
lived - a holy and righteous life - and you have been called
to proclaim the gospel of Christ to a world lost and reeling
under the weight of enormous need.
*Acts 20:28; 1 Corinthians 6:19-20*

## 4. You are counted faithful - counted trustworthy - by Christ.

This is a most wonderful thought, that Christ Jesus counts
you trustworthy (I Tim. 1:12). He trusts you to be faithful,
and in the final analysis, He knows that you will be faithful
to Him. This is one of the reasons He has chosen you and
put you into the ministry.

Note the word "enabled." It means strength and power.
The power of your ministry comes from Christ. Christ
gives you the power to minister and to conquer all. You
must always remember this:
• *No matter what may confront you or how far down*
*you may fall, Christ counts you faithful and Christ will*
*give you the power to be faithful. Christ knows that you*
*will arise and begin to serve with renewed fervor.*

This is the reason Christ called you: because in the final
analysis you will be faithful. How can you know and be
assured of this? Because of the forgiveness and the power
and faithfulness of Christ. Christ will lift you up. Therefore when you fall, you must arise and seek the forgiveness

2

of Christ and begin to walk anew in the strength and power
of Christ.
*1 Timothy 1:12; 1 Corinthians 4:2; Colossians 1:25; Isaiah
6:8*

## THE MINISTER WITHIN HIMSELF

It goes without saying that the minister is a Christian, and
goes with this saying that he is a gentleman. This is the
base line of code assembled in this message. It is accepted
as an axiom that every minister is a Christian gentleman.

By common consent the Christian ministry is esteemed the
noblest of the professions. Some may object to this classi-
fication, and some may wish it qualified by affirming that
by the Christian ministry is meant a real ministry and not a
counterfeit one.

General consent, however, does give to the ministry prima-
cy among the noble callings. If this much is accorded by
persons other than the minister, he himself certainly ought
to hold his profession in as high regard as does the world.
Many ministers believe it to be higher in kind as well as
degree, but they never press these upon others. They take
the recognition of their "higher calling," not as a mark of
personal honor to themselves, but as an honor to that one
who first called them. Like the Apostle, the best minister
strives to apprehend that for which he was himself appre-
hended.

From this acknowledged truth that the ministry is the highest form of professional service sprung several principles
that form the axioms on which any consideration of the
minister's conduct must be based:

**1. The minister must keep the nobility of his calling uppermost in his own mind.**
Should he fail to do this, he had better take up some other form of work. If for any cause he begins to look down upon his profession, or to feel that for him its glory has departed, he is lost. The temptation comes to him, for instance, to measure the ministry by some of the standards which apply to the work of other professions. The professional standard of the ministry belong to another category, a spiritual one, nevertheless a very real one. The Christian ministry cannot be measured by the financial standard.

**2. The minister must hold high in outward acts for establishing reputation of the Christian ministry.**
There is a popular esteem in which the ministry is held, a popular regard, estimation, and measure, not the making of one generation but of all generations. It is entirely possible for someone minister to lower or injure this popular estimation. Conduct unbecoming a gentleman is always conduct unbecoming a minister.

**3. The minister must never forget that he is one who serves . . . And that he must be on guard against a temptation which his very profession presents to him.**
He occupies a position in the local church and congregation which puts him upon a pedestal in the minds of the people. Everything serves to dramatize the centrality of his place as a pastor, a preacher, an executive, and long continued and unchallenged leadership often intensifies this preeminence. Never misuse the power and influence you have accumulated.

**4. The minister must never, for reasons of personal safety, desert his parish and people when some great, universal danger impends.**

You are called to be the shepherd of the flock. Being a shepherd involves danger from within and from without.

### 5. The minister must utilize his time properly.
Like other professions, the ministry is not a matter of eight working hours with pay-and-a-half for overtime, but of life service. The minister therefore gives himself completely to his profession.

### 6. The minister must never measure his work by the salary involved.
It is the just pride of all the professions that they place service before profit, but no matter what may be the case with others; this rule may never be forgotten nor deviated from by the ministry.

### 7. The minister must guard the use of his name.
He should not give the sanction of his endorsement to those causes or movement of which he cannot be sure. Men and women of prominence, ministers among them, have often had cause to regret the fact that they permitted their names to be used on the letterhead of supposedly charitable or benevolent organization.

### 8. The minister must not lower his profession by becoming a "handy man" for all the members of the church.

### 9. The minister must hold his professional service in such esteem that he will keep it from being dissipated in the maze of shallow channels of service which open out in all directions.

### 10. The minister should deal honestly with his financial obligation.
There is one inflexible duty which the minister owes to himself, to his family, to his profession, and to his church-

he must be absolutely exact on money matters. Financial looseness or irregularity cannot be tolerated. All the preaching a man may do will not atone for unpaid bills. He may have what is to a good excuse, but in the eyes of the world there is no excuse for failure to pay debts. You must be aware the damage can be done by borrowing money from members and even the church. You cannot pastor those whom you owe.

# PROTECTING AND PROMOTING YOUR PASTOR

*Protect* to defend or guard from attack, invasion, loss, annoyance, insult, etc.; cover or shield from injury or danger.

*Promote*: to help or encourage existing or flourishing; further to aid in organizing.

**A Model Armor Bearer**
1 Samuel 14:1-15

_____

_____

**He was Devoted**
1 Samuel 14:6-7; Proverbs 25:19

_____

_____

**He was Daring**
1 Samuel 14:8-11

_____

_____

**He was Detailed**
1 Samuel 14:13-14

---

---

**The Servant of Moses**
Exodus 24:13; Joshua 1:1; Exodus 17:8-14

---

---

**Servant hood Development**

---

---

**Protect His Time and Energy**
Acts 6:4; Acts 6:19; Acts 6:2-4

---

---

**Do not be a Garbage Receptacle**
1 Timothy 5:19; Proverbs 26:21

---

---

**Do not be a pit bull**

---

---

**Do not join with the sharks**
Galatians 6:1; 1 Timothy 5:19-20

---

---

# The Tragedy of Being Uncoachable
"Rare Air" By Michael Jordan

**Teamwork not individual talent wins championships**
Ephesians 4:12; Luke 6:40; Matthew 4:21

---

---

**Shows up late for practice or doesn't show up at all**

---

**Won't do what is necessary in order to stay in shape**

---

**Listens to the fans instead of the coach**
Hebrews 13:17

---

---

**Aaron's Dilemma:**
**What To Do When Your Leader is Away?**

**Complete Your Assignment**
Mark 13:34-37

---

---

**Don't Fall Asleep**
Matthew 23:24-25

---

**What not to do while Pastor is Away**
Exodus 32:1-4; Exodus 24:14

---

---

**Aaron let the people run wild**
Exodus 32:25

_____

_____


**Aaron would not take responsibility for his actions**
Luke 12:42-48

_____

_____

# YOUNG MINISTERS PITFALLS

The ministerial pathway is beset with many hidden pitfalls for young ministers. Any minister would be wise to recognize these pitfalls. Since the minister must live in a glass house, not even his most secret pitfall can be hidden from the all-seeing of curious members of his congregation. They are there. Why not face them and do something about them? Let's look together, and honestly, at a few of these pitfalls.

1. One of the greatest danger-point for a young preacher is to have an unduly exalted opinion of himself. Like any other human being, a young preacher may feel that he is the most important person in the world. This exalted position may be formed and fed by commendations from members of the congregation who commend the minister, not for what he already is, but for what they earnestly hope and pray he may yet become if grace abounds and the church can endure. A young preacher's sermon is his apple pie, and he sometimes wonders how his church was able to survive before he began to preach such wonderful sermons. He wonders how other churches have such large congregations without the benefit of his type of preaching.

2. A second pitfall for a young preacher is the assumption of disparaging attitude toward other ministers. It is a common sin among preachers to disparage their predecessors in the pastorate. Either directly or by implication, many preachers discredit the former pastor by magnifying the progress, growth and improvements "since I came." Another common weapon of disparagement is the habit of blueprinting the weakness and faults of the church "when I came." Veteran deacons and older church members, who have weathered the storms of ages and have been found

faithful, frequently become the victims of disparagements. The minister himself creates many crises.

3. Many ministers are snared into pitfalls when they become glory seeking, honor and power crazy. Many will seek to destroy other ministers thinking that will help them to become the accepted leader. Whom the Lord raises and promotes no man can hinder. (Haman and Mordecai) (Joseph and his brethren).

4. Another pitfall for ministers is the impulse to **"Get Them Told."** Yes, they do need telling, but the telling needs to be done in a spirit of humility and love. It is the preacher who gets them told in the wrong way that finds himself in great difficulty. **"Getting them told"** has unnecessarily driven many ministers from their pastorates.

5. The desire to clean out the church is another pitfall. You didn't clutter it up, is it your business to clean it out? God didn't call you to stir up the stench of the gutter. He didn't call you to drag skeletons out of the closets. Yes, it is obvious that many churches do need to have a house cleaning, but if they are to be cleaned, let the church do it. God did not call preachers to be house cleaners, but house builders. You are not to be the arresting officer, but you are the judge.

6. The pitfall of being swayed by every kind of doctrine. Pastors and preachers need to know what they believe and why they believe it. A church doesn't mind following a man who knows where he is going. (Eph 4:14). (I Cor. 15:58).

# FINDING BALANCE IN YOUR MINISTRY

Stress multiplies when we try to balance too many activities and obligations at one time. You wonder *How I can be true to myself, my Lord, my church, my family, and my financial obligations.* Just as our automobiles need to undergo regular maintenance checks in order to run smoothly, perhaps we should consider regular "life" checks to help us balance four major obligations: our personal lives, our professions, our families, and our finances.

**1. Be true to yourself.** Life is a journey of discovery. We often become so concerned about others that we don't take time to discover ourselves. Use this list to inventory your qualities and discover how you might be inadvertently contributing to your stress.

*Know Your Unique Personality Type*
Could you be causing yourself stress because you're trying to be someone you're not? Consider these personality differences:

- Do you need to talk about your problems with someone, or do you prefer time alone to think?
- Are you a "possibility thinker" who considers life in terms of what could be, or a "reality, bottom-line thinker" who considers life in terms of what is?
- Do you approach a decision with your head or with your heart?
- Do you plan your work and work your plan, or do you go with the flow?

God makes and uses people with all of these traits. Understanding and accepting your personality can help you eliminate the stress of guilt. Be who you are (and surround yourself with people who make up for who and what you aren't).

### Know Your Gifts and Talents
God blessed you with a unique blend of gifts and talents. If you try to spend 60 percent of your time in your gifted areas, you will feel successful more than half the time! That successful feeling will give you the energy to face the other 40 percent.

### Know Your Energy Cycles
Take note of your energy levels throughout the day and the week.
- Which day of the week are you most energized and productive?
- What time of the day are you most alert and able to accomplish the most?

Plan your most creative work at that time. You can sabotage your productivity by trying to do your best work when you are not at your best.

### Know Your Life Stage
If you understand that some of your stress comes along with the stage of life you're in, it may be easier to embrace the stage rather than using your energy to fight it. For example, here are some things to keep in mind when you're in difficult stages of pastoral life:
- Graduate school will end.
- The children will not always be underfoot.
- Midlife is a good time to stop and ask, *Is what I am doing working? How well am I suited for this role? Do I want to do this the rest of my life? Is God calling me to do something else?*
- Retirement may offer opportunities to travel, to relax, or to serve the Lord in new ways.

### Know Your Limitations

Only God can do everything. You have limits. Figure out what they are, and learn to say occasionally, "I just can't do that right now." Choose what you will do based on importance, not on urgency.

### Know What a "Sabbath" Means

God guilt in us a rhythm of productivity. We will function best if every seven days or so we pause for a time of rest, reflection, renewal, and energizing. Also consider a few minutes of "Sabbath" when you are feeling really stressed or weary. You are not a machine and as such, your body requires rest. Do not make the misinterpretation that attending a convention is a vacation as many ministers often times do.

### Know Your God

Have you allowed the work of the Lord to take the place of the Lord of the work? If so, ask for God's forgiveness and allow him to redirect your efforts. It is also helpful to seek godly counsel from a trusted friend or mentor. Everybody needs somebody that they can turn to for help.

### Know Your Hot Buttons and How They Are Pushed

What sets you off? When does the stress seem unbearable? Are there any patterns? Could it be you are carrying unfinished business from the past into the present situation? You might consider seeing a counselor to help you explore any unhealthy patterns.

### Know How to Handle Conflict

What's your attitude toward conflict? Does it energize you? Paralyze you with fear? Make you want to quit...fight...avoid it? Conflict and chaos are the labor pains of new birth. The three men walked with God in the fiery furnace; resurrection came after the cross; the first deacons were chosen after a church fight; Gentiles were included in the good news after Peter and Paul struggled to help other church leaders open their minds! We can grow from conflict.

*Ask a Friend to Keep You Accountable*
Do you have a friend who is not a part of your church and not a relative, someone who will allow you to be honest and open? Is there someone in your life who knows your dreams and can remind you when you are getting out of balance?

## 2. Manage on-the-job Stress
Ministry is never finished! It has been going on since the days of the Old Testament and will continue long after we are gone. There will always be people in crisis, pastoral calls to make, sermons to write, more expenses than income. Sometimes you need an attitude adjustment, other times you need new systems of organization, and still other times you need to just let go. Gaining insights in the following areas could help you keep your balance:

*Know What Drains You and What Energizes You*
A 50-hour week of worship preparation and visiting the homebound probably takes less out of you than 30-hours that include preparing the funeral service of a young mother who has left three small children; calling on a member whose son has just been caught with drugs; and leading a board meeting full of disputes, confusion, and chaos. Give yourself permission to rest after draining experiences. Know that if you permit stress to take you out, the church will mourn for thirty days and move on as if nothing has happened so you must take the lead in getting the appropriate amount of rest and recuperation.

*Know Your Priorities*
What are the most important things you have to do? Do you keep these tasks at the top of your "To Do" list? There's a difference between urgent and important. If we respond only to the urgent, we'll never get to the important! Interruptions can be urgent or important; try to discern which is which.

*Know How to Keep a Calendar*
Do you have a system that helps you stay organized? On your calendar note important things like exercise, dates with your spouse, and prayer time. When someone calls and asks if you're doing anything, you can answer "Yes!" It is important to note here that you should only keep one calendar that identifies everything that you need and want to attend. Having a calendar at home, on your phone and at the church can prove to be counterproductive when you forget to transfer the data accordingly.

*Know How to Plan*
Church life has a seasonal cycle. Think quarterly. While implementing the present season's plans, be planning at least for the next season's events. You can reduce stress if you spend a nearly equal amount of time each week in the implementation of plans and in the development of plans. After a particularly exhausting flurry of activity, you and your leaders will need a time of rest. The week after Easter or Christmas is not a good time to do intense training, but it is a great time to kick back!

*Know How to Communicate*
Have you developed systems that enable people to get the information they need? Is your mode of communication effective? As the leader, what is your style of communication? Is it working?

*Know How to Anticipate Your Next Step*
What do you need to know to take the next significant step forward in ministry? Where do you need to fill gaps in personnel and in insight? Don't recruit people who know only what you know; expand your pool of insight by gathering people around you who have others gifts and expertise.

*Know Whose Church It Really Is*
Remember that God is in control. When things aren't going well, trust him, not your own abilities.

## 3. Keep the Home Fires Burning
Other ministers can lead your congregation, but no one can take your place in your family. You have a unique ministry to your wife and children. At the end of your life, you will not regret missing a meeting at the church, but you will regret time you didn't spend with your family. To reduce stress in the home, consider the following principles.

*Know How to Leave the Church When You Walk in the House*
Can you truly be fully present in the present? Make a "to do" list before you leave the church and leave the list on your desk as a concrete way to leave church matters at the church. Your mind won't have to keep track of it as long as it is on the list!

*Know Your Spouse*
If you're married, do you remember why you married your spouse? After the children are grown and you retire from professional church work, your relationship with your spouse will still be intact if you have consistently invested time in your spouse.

### Know Your Children

If you have children, spend quality time with them. This means doing activities that interest your children. However, children can also share in your ministry time. For example, take them along when you visit the shut-in. Invite your children to ride to the hospital with you; then share a burger with them at Burger King. But don't make the mistake of thinking that "quality time" can make up for too little time. Remember, too, that the best way to love your children is to love their other parent.

### Know Re-energizing Friends

Do you have friends who help fill your cup? Do your friends lift you up or bring you down? Look for friends who don't always need you to minister to them. Make sure someone in your life can minister to you.

### Know How to Laugh

When was the last time you enjoyed a good belly laugh? "A merry heart doeth good like medicine" (Proverbs 17:22). Laughter actually produces endorphins that stimulate a good mood even if you've been feeling stressed or down.

### Know How to Love

Have you and your spouse created an environment that fosters love and affection? Is God's grace present in your home? If we can't show love at home, how will they "know we are Christians by our love"?

## 4. Put Your Finances to the Test

Money is rarely the root of our stress; rather, it is our attitude toward money that usually causes stress. When it came to material things, Paul wrote that he had learned to be content (Philippians 4:11-13). It takes money to live, but have you noticed that the more money you make, the more it takes to live? Photocopy and fill in this chart and then take the steps described in the following chart to help you face the reality of your financial stress.

*Know Your Income*
_____ your monthly income from the church
_____ your spouse's monthly income
_____ other monthly income (weddings, funerals, speaking engagements)
_____ other income such as Social Security and child support
_____ allowances and benefits such as housing allowance and insurance premiums

*Know How to Budget Monthly Expenses*

| | | | |
|---|---|---|---|
| _____ | tithe | _____ | savings |
| _____ | car payments | _____ | fuel for vehicles |
| _____ | food | _____ | clothes |
| _____ | mortgage | _____ | heat |
| _____ | electric | _____ | water |
| _____ | phone | _____ | trash |
| _____ | other (discretionary expenses) | | |

*Know How to Anticipate Expenses That Aren't Monthly*
Estimate the cost for a year and divide by 12.
_____ self-employment taxes
_____ car repairs/maintenance
_____ medical expenses
_____ car/life/house insurance
_____ property tax
_____ vacations

Add up your total income and your total expenses. Do your expenses exceed your income? How much stress does that add to your life? Look for ways to cut back expenses or to increase household income.

*Know How to Give*
If you and your spouse both work, you might use the larger of the two incomes to tithe to your church and a portion of the smaller income to use as "God's play money"— resources you keep on hand to give to people in need or support individuals you know, such as short-term missionaries. Teach your children the thrill of giving. Don't give until it hurts; give until it feels good.

*Know How to Receive*
Do you know how to graciously receive gifts from others? Allow others the blessing of giving to you.

*Know How to Ask God for Help*
God knows your needs, but he still wants you to talk to him.

# Chapter 2 Leadership Through Excellence

## FROM FOLLOWSHIP TO LEADERSHIP
## COURSE OUTLINE

*Whoever wants to become great among you must be your servant, and whomever wants to be first must be slave of all.* **Mark 10:43-44**

1.  Characteristics of a Good Follower
    A. Humble
    B. Trustworthy
    C. Supporter of the Vision
    D. Powerful Prayer Life
    E. Dependable

2.  What is a Leader?
    A. A Leader is Not
        1. An office or position
        2. A rule-maker
        3. A speech maker
        4. A manager
        5. An administrator or organizer

    B. A Leader
        1. Is humble in the use of authority and power entrusted to them.
        2. Is trustworthy with a lot of integrity.
        3. Is willing to lead out of leadership gifting and ability rather than their leadership position
        4. Uses a style of leadership that seeks to love and serve others and God
        5. Shares the vision of the church

# DEFINING LEADERSHIP

Leadership is the art of motivating a group of people to act towards achieving a common goal.

Put even more simply, the leader is the inspiration and director of the action. He or she is the person in the group that possesses the combination of personality and skills that makes others want to follow his or her direction. Leadership is welded to performance. Effective leaders are those who increase the Association's bottom lines.

Leadership is the process of social influence in which once person can enlist the aid and support of others in the accomplishment of a common task.

Leadership is the ability to lead.

Leadership is the development of a vision and strategies; the alignment of relevant people behind these strategies, and the empowerment of individuals to make the vision happen despite obstacles.

Ann Marie E. McSwain, Assistant Professor at Lincoln University states "Leadership is about capacity: the capacity of leaders to listen and observe, to use their expertise as a starting point to encourage dialogue between all levels of decision-making, to establish processes and transparency in decision-making, to articulate their own values and visions clearly but not impose them. Leadership is about setting and not just reacting to agendas, identifying problems, and initiating change that makes for substantive improvement rather than managing change."

John C. Maxwell defines leadership as "leadership is influence - nothing more, nothing less."

Warren Bennis defined leadership saying "Leadership is a function of knowing yourself, having a vision that is well communicated, building trust among colleagues, and taking effective action to realize your own leadership potential.

Effective leadership is the ability to successfully integrate and maximize available resources within the internal and external environment for the attainment of organizational or societal goals.

## LEADERSHIP TYPES

### 1. Charismatic Leadership
Charismatic Leadership is a term that became known in the management field initially with the work of a German sociologist Max Weber. He described certain leaders as having exceptional qualities (a charisma) that enabled them to motivate followers to achieve outstanding performance. *Charisma* is Greek word meaning "gift bestowed by the gods." Robert House uses four phrases to define charismatic leadership:
- Dominant
- Strong desire to influence others
- Self-confident
- Strong sense of one's own moral values

Jay Conger proposed the following four-stage model of charismatic leadership:

1. Continual assessment of the environment to formulate what must be done; establishes goals
2. Communication of his or her vision; uses motivational and persuasive arguments
3. Building trust and commitment; unexpected behavior, risk-taking; technical proficiency
4. Role modeling, empowerment, and unconventional tactics

Charismatic leaders are generally spurred to action by ideology and vision, or by crisis. They usually take on hero status with their followers, employees, and sometimes nations. The dangers, however, with this style of leadership, may include extreme need for control over others and dependent followers.

There are several personal weaknesses of charismatic leaders can cause failure with this leadership style. Charismatic leaders can tend to possess narcissistic tendencies and fail to delegate their responsibilities and authority to subordinates. Because of their unpredictability and insensitivity to others, these leaders can also be harmful to their followers.

## 2. Transformational Leadership
Transformational leadership enhances the motivation, morale and performance of followers through a variety of mechanisms including connecting the follower's sense of identity and self to the mission and the collective identity of the organization; being a role model for followers that inspires them; challenging followers to take greater ownership for their work, and understanding the strengths and weaknesses of followers, so the leader can align followers with tasks that optimize their performance.

James MacGregor Burns first introduce the concept of transforming leadership in his descriptive research on political leaders, but this term is now used in organizational psychology as well. According to Burns, transforming leadership is a process in which "leaders and followers help each other to advance to a higher level of morale and motivation". He related to the difficulty in differentiation between management and leadership and claimed that the differences are in characteristics and behaviors.

Transforming leadership creates significant change in the life of people and organizations. It redesigns perceptions and values, and changes expectations and aspirations of employees. It is not based on a "give and take" relationship, but on the leader's personality, traits and ability to make a change through example, articulation of an energizing vision and challenging goals. Transforming leaders are idealized in the sense that they are a moral exemplar of working towards the benefit of the team, organization and/or community.

When the Bible talks about transformational leadership, it discusses the "being" transformed as a model to be reproduced within an organism, as is the church. As a basic premise for transformation, the Bible encourages transformed leaders to experience the invitation to transform the world around them. With this end in mind, there are three basic assumptions about transformation:

a. **Assumption #1:** The Lord Jesus Christ's main purpose of presence is to transform the world through transformed people. (Matthew 4:19) Not, followers, but leaders.

b. **Assumption #2:** God's only means for Global transformation was and is through transformed individuals. (Matthew 5:13-14)

    **c. Assumption #3**: Transformed followers of Jesus Christ passionately engage in displaying the transforming power of the gospel locally and globally.

A review of the gospel writings depicts Jesus being committed to leading a group of transformed followers who followed Him to learn the art of transforming communities of people. The goal of transformational leaders is to lead of a group of transformed individuals who in turn will learn the art of transforming their communities and the world. Their mission: to follow the transformational model of Jesus Christ.

The leaders of the New Testament acted similar to Jesus Christ in that they immolated Christ in five core practices:

**1. His practice of spiritual and relational vitality.**
A. Encountering God's holiness (Isaiah 6:1-4)
B. Experiencing God's grace (Isaiah 6:5-8)
C. Embracing unity in authentic Christian community (Eph. 4:1-3)
D. Engaging community through transformed Christlike followers

**2. His ability to establish a core of followers**
Jesus used His influence and character to create an environment for reproduction. Jesus' character harmonized with who He was. This enabled Him to build a following based on His capacity to demonstrate personal transformation.

**3. His ability to engage and influence the core in reproducing His purpose.**
Jesus influenced His followers to participate in His mission. John Maxwell developed a working model that illustrates the five level of influence:

- Level One: **Position** - (Rights) People follow because they have to
- Level Two: **Permission or Personal Relationships** - (Relationships) People follow because they want to
- Level Three: **Production** - (Results) People follow because of what you are able to achieve for the organization
- Level Four: **People Development** - (Reproduction) People follow because of what you have done for them
- Level Five: **Personhood** - (Respect) People follow you because of who you are and what you represent

Jesus demonstrated all five of these levels of leadership as a means of engaging followers in establishing a vision community of leaders. They follow Jesus with the knowledge of His position as the Lamb of God (John 1:35-37). To establish relational vitality among His followers, Jesus invited them to His home (John 1:38-39). Throughout His ministry Jesus developed relational capital with His followers. As a leader, He demonstrated the ability to produce results. This caused His followers to express the desire to embrace His vision (Luke 5:1-11).

Growth occurred when He spent personal time and effort to develop them (Matthew 4:18-19). When there was creative tension among His followers towards the vision, they continued to embrace the vision based upon His personhood (John 6:59-69). As we study the life of Jesus in the gospels, we discover the art of turning followers into leaders. This is at the heart of transformational leadership.

**4. His ability to achieving and maintaining widespread impact cultivating and empowering followers into leaders.**

To achieve and maintain impact and empowerment of followers into leaders, it requires 3 important elements:

a. Establishment of a new model for leadership within the core. A new definition for leadership that helps in the process of turning followers into leaders would be: A leader is a **Person** who influences **People** to **Participate** in a God given **Purpose**.

b. Empower leaders by creating a sense of urgency. (Matthew 5-7)

c. Removing obstacles that prohibit transformational values. Putting the right people on the right bus, in the right seat and going in the right direction, helps to sustain the right vision.

**5. His ability to encourage the core to create an eye on their community to expand the vision community of reproducible followers.**

Transformational leaders must develop the skills of discovering their mission field based upon who and what they are. This is quite different from the western model for church growth where believers are extracted from the world from which they live and connect, to participate in the institution's ministry objectives. The existents of the believer's ministry evolve within the context of the local church geographically and as well as institutionally. In Mark 5:1-21, Jesus encouraged a man to create an eye for his community to expand the vision community of reproducible followers. In a rapid period of time, the man became part of the vision for rapid reproduction.

## 3. Transactional Leadership

Transactional leadership is a term used to classify a formally known group leadership theories that inquire the interactions between leaders and followers. A transactional leader focuses more on a series of "transactions." This person is interested in looking out for oneself, having exchange benefits with their subordinates and clarifies a sense of duty with rewards and punishments to reach goals.

Transactional leaders help the subordinate identify what must be done to achieve the goal. Though the exchange process may sometimes appear simplistic, as a paycheck for work, theories of transactional leadership can be complex and include the leader helping the subordinate identify what must be done as well what might motivate the follower to succeed.

Because Christianity offers eternal rewards, church leaders should offer rewards that move to the eternal level. The souls of man and women are eternal where all other rewards are temporal. When you set your follower's sights on eternal values, you can offer rewards that non-religious organizations can't complete with.

Ministry, as in any other church work, should be postured as rewarding work. It is no shame to motivate people reminding them of the great rewards they will receive by volunteering to work in the nursery, or go on the youth retreat as a counselor. While few Christians may actually work for the reward, knowledge of the rewards may provide additional motivation for volunteers in the church.

Thus, church leaders should intentionally outline the rewards and benefits of church work and intentionally sell the value of church volunteering as part of their comprehensive volunteer recruitment strategy.

### 4. Servant Leadership
Servant leadership is a philosophy and practice of leadership as coined and defined by Robert Greenleaf. Servant-leaders achieve results for their organizations by giving priority attention to the needs of their colleagues and those they serve. They are often viewed as humble stewards of their organization's resources (human, financial and physical).

The philosophy of leading by serving has been explained by countless leadership theorists to include building an environment that not only serves the needs of the organization, but also provides a climate for its workers to grow and develop as human beings.

A functional definition of servant leaders and servant-led organizations developed by Dr. James Alan Laub using the Delphi method would be that servant leaders and servant-led organizations

- **Value People** - by believing in people, putting others first and by listening
- **Develop People** - by developing potential, modeling appropriate behavior and encouraging others
- **Build Community** - by enhancing relationships, emphasizing teamwork and valuing the differing gifts, cultures, and viewpoints of others
- **Display Authenticity** - by being transparent, self-aware and open to input from others and by maintaining integrity
- **Provide Leadership** - by envisioning the future, moving out ahead through initiative and by clarifying goals

- **Share Leadership** - by empowering others and sharing status

There are several qualities that one must possess in order to be a servant leader:
- Listening
- Empathy
- Healing
- Awareness
- Persuasion
- Conceptualization
- Foresight
- Stewardship
- Growth
- Building community

Jesus urged his followers to be servants first. (Matthew 20:25-28; also Mark 10:42-45). He also washed the feet of his disciples, as an example of the way in which they were to serve each other. (John 13:12-15)

## WHAT LEADERS DO?

1. Provide purpose and direction - Mission, Vision and Goals.

2. Lead in strategy formulation

3. Mobilize people and resources and empower others to support and achieve the vision.

4. Change from "status-quo" to the desired future

5. Take critical decisions and actions, and solve major problems.

6. Attract, train, motivate and develop other leaders and managers

7. Motivate

8. Act as models

9. Minister to other's needs (Serve)

10. Mentor people to bring out the best in them.

## WHAT IS SPIRITUAL LEADERSHIP?

Spiritual leadership is defined as moving people onto God's agenda. An alternate definition is God-directed influence. Spiritual leaders must be led by God before leading others in God's name. It is important for spiritual leaders to never gather followers to themselves but followers after God.

### John Piper on Spiritual Leadership
I define spiritual leadership as knowing where God wants people to be and taking the initiative to use God's methods to get them there in reliance on God's power. The answer to where God wants people to be is in a spiritual condition and in a lifestyle that displays his glory and honors his name. Therefore, the goal of spiritual leadership is that people come to know God and to glorify him in all that they do. Spiritual leadership is aimed not so much at directing people as it is at changing people. If we would be the kind of leaders we ought to be, we must make it our aim to develop persons rather than dictate plans. You can get people to do what you want, but if they don't change in their heart you have not led them spiritually. You have not taken them to where God wants them to be.

### 1. A Calling.
Holding a leadership position in a Christian organization does not make one a spiritual leader. Spiritual leadership is not an occupation: it is a calling.

### 2. Leaders You Can Trust
People know intuitively that claiming to be a leader or holding a leadership position does not make someone a leader. People are warily looking for leaders they can trust.

### 3. Leadership Based on Scripture
The trend among Christian leaders has been for an almost indiscriminate and uncritical acceptance of secular leadership theory without measuring it against the timeless precepts of Scripture.

### 4. God's Authority in the Spiritual and Secular Realm
The problem was the Israelites' assumptions that spiritual concerns, such as righteous living and obedience to God, belonged in the religious realm while the practical issues of doing battle with enemies, strengthening the economy, and unifying the country were secular matters. They forgot that God himself had won their military victories, brought them prosperity, and created their nation. He was as active on the battlefield as he was in the worship service. When the

Israelites separated spiritual concerns from political and economic issues, their nation was brought to its knees. Scripture indicates that it is a mistake to separate the spiritual world from the secular world.

## 5. God's Leading for Leaders.
Spiritual leadership is not restricted to pastors and missionaries. It is the responsibility of all Christians whom God wants to use to make a difference in their world. The challenge for today's leaders is to discern the difference between the latest leadership fads and timeless truths established by God.

## 6. God's Agenda
There a number of helpful definitions of leadership available, but we believe true spiritual leadership can be defined in one concise statement: Spiritual leadership is moving people on to God's agenda.

## 7. Valuable Model of Leadership
Too often leaders allow secular models of leadership to corrupt the straightforward model set forth by Jesus.

## 8. Leading Through Obedience
Jesus has established the model for Christian leaders. It is not found in his 'methodology.' Rather, it is seen in his absolute obedience to the Father's will.

O=Obey the Calling
B=Begin a study
E=Examine feelings and fantasies
D=Disciplined Belief
I=Investigate the Gifts of Others
E=Experiment with the Gifts
N=Never doubt God's promises
C=Censure all notions of pride and defeat
E=Expect God to produce the results

## 9. Look and Listen to the Father
If Jesus provides the model for spiritual leadership, then the key is not for leaders to develop visions and to set the direction for their organizations. The key is to obey and to preserve everything the Father

reveals to them of his will.

### 10. Pleasing God
Spiritual leaders do not try to satisfy the goals and ambitions of the people they lead but those of the God they serve.

### 11. Seeking and Acting
Spiritual leaders seek God's will, whether it is for their church (mission) or for their corporation, and then they marshal their people to pursue God's plan.

### 12. Being Christ-Like
Just as Christians are aware that a worldly lifestyle can discredit their Christian witness to others, so leaders know that a careless lifestyle can diminish their credibility in the eyes of their followers.

## SECULAR LEADERSHIP VS SPIRITUAL LEADERSHIP

Leadership in the Church is completely different and separate from the world. You cannot and must not think that the two are interchangeable because they are not. Although the two share common issues, the responses are different.

### 1. How to gain influence?
It is a common concern that leaders are those who have influence over others. In the world, we view leaders show influence by leveraging power over others. It is important to understand that the Church is different. Christ did not call us to lord over the people but to shepherd and lead them. The scripture teaches us that in order to effectively influence others, we first must love people.
*Philippians 2:3-11*

### 2. How to possess confidence?
People want to follow someone who is confident in their message. Leaders in the corporate market gain confidence by viewing the world as a "dog eat dog" world. In order to be successful, one must compete with others in order to get ahead. Again, the scripture teaches us a better way. Church leaders must depend on God if they desire con-

fidence.
*2 Corinthians 3:4-6*

### 3. How to acquire authority?
As ministers and Christian leaders, we must never try to usurp authority over the Church. It is the world that requires a person to claim their rights and position in order to display their authority. Your authority comes only by servant hood. Remember that God called you serve, not be served.
*Matthew 20:20-28*

### 4. How to grow an organization?
Secular organizations demand different things of people in order to grow. But in order for the Church to grow, it must develop people instead. The same thing applies to our ministry. It is good that God has chosen us to work for Him in growing the Church. If you ever get to the point where people are no longer important to you, then you have failed in this aspect.
*Acts 19:8-10*

### 5. What vision drives you?
Do you know what it is that drives you to do what it is that you do? On your job, it's temporal gain such as your paycheck or even a promotion. Many ministers fall short by equating their ministry with the gifts people share with them. It is better to remind yourself that your reward is in Heaven. When you do this, it won't matter to you that people didn't say "Amen" while you were preaching or they didn't pay you the honorarium you thought you deserved.
*Matthew 6:31-32*

### 6. What is success?
How do you measure success? The world paints the picture of a successful person having completed schooling, great job making $40K or more a year and a happy marriage with a successful spouse. In the secular realm, you become successful by overcoming the competition by outdoing everyone else. Don't fall snare to this in the Church. As a minister, if no one else understands the concept of success, you should know that the Word of God has given you a roadmap to suc-

cess. True success can only come from obeying God.
*1 Corinthians 4:1-5*

**7. The heart of leadership**
In the world, you work for a boss who is at the head of the food chain. You view this individual as such and nothing else. However, as Christians we know that at the heart of leadership, we have a Father that we can share all of our burdens and heartaches with.
*1 Corinthians 4:15*

# THE MEANING OF CHURCH LEADERSHIP

**LOYAL**

A leader sets an example in loyalty to the whole church program.

**ENTERPRISING**

A leader is industrious and sees through or around difficulties. He does not mind working hard and sacrificially.

**ATTENTIVE**

A leader gives close attention to details, remembering that "cursed is he that doeth the work of the Lord negligently."

**DEPENDABLE**

A leader is always ready and on time. He is always present not only for the service for which he is responsible but for all services.

**EAGER**

A leader is enthusiastic about serving the Lord in the position which he has been elected.

**RADIANT**

A leader is happy and optimistic, seldom criticizing and always encouraging others.

**SURRENDERED**

A leader puts Christ first; others second, and himself last.

| | |
|---|---|
| **HONEST** | A leader gives at least one-seventh of his time and one-tenth of his money to the Lord through his church. |
| **INTEGRITY** | A leader does the right thing even when there is no one else around. |
| **PASSIONATE** | A leader is passionate about his craft and will always strive to perfect it. |

# CHURCH LEADERSHIP

I.    Whoever wants to become great among you must be your servant and whoever wants to be first must be a slave to all.
Mark 10:43, 44

II.    Christian Leadership - Ability given by God to certain Christians to provide motivation for people and get them to follow with the accomplishment of a common goal in mind.

III.    Eight Laws of Leadership

    1.   People follow a leader who directs them to a desirable objective.
    2.   People follow a leader who provides the rewards from their self-chosen goals.
    3.   People follow a leader when they have confidence in his/her plan to reach the objective.
    4.   People follow a leader who effectively communicates his/her plan to reach the objective.
    5.   People follow a leader who gives them a responsibility to help reach the objective.
    6.   People follow a leader who gives them compelling rea-

sons to reach the objective.

7. People follow a leader who gives solutions to problems that hinder them from reaching the objective.

8. People follow a leader who gives answers to the decisions involving their objectives.

IV. The best test of whether one is a qualified leader is to find out whether anyone is following him.

V. He who thinketh he leadeth and no one is following is just taking a walk.

VI. Ineffective leadership is over-come through training, opportunities to lead, and leadership empowerment.

VII. Ineffective leadership should never be allowed to become an established part of the church.

## BEATITUDES FOR CHURCH LEADERS

Blessed is the leader who has not sought the highest places but who has been drafted into them because of his ability and willingness to serve.

Blessed is the leader who knows where he is going, why he is going and how to get there.

Blessed is the leader who knows no discouragement and presents no alibi.

Blessed is the leader who can lead without being dictatorial.

Blessed is the leader who seeks the best for those whom he serves.

Blessed is the leader who leads for the food of the majority and not for himself.

Blessed is the leader who marches with the group and interprets the signs that lead to success.

Blessed is the leader who considers leadership to be Christian service.

Blessed is the leader who is eager to train for his office.

## THE "5" PRINCIPLES OF POTENTIAL

*Potential is what you're capable of doing, Motivation determines what you do, but your Character and Attitude determine how well you do it.*

1. Your released potential is the world's inheritance.
2. You came into the world pregnant with unlimited potential.
3. You are capable of much more than you have already done.
4. Creation's destiny is tied to the release of your potential.
5. The fact that you were born is evidence that God knew earth need-ed the potential you are pregnant with.

*"God's gift to us is potential. When we maximize our potential, it's our gift back to God."*                                              - Dr. Frank
A. White

## THE TEN COMMANDMENTS OF HOW TO GET ALONG WITH PEOPLE

1. Keep skid chains on your tongue. Always say less than you think. Cultivate a low persuasive voice. How you say it often counts more than what you say.

2. Make promises sparingly and keep them faithfully, no matter what

the cost.

3. Never let an opportunity pass to say a kind and encouraging word to or about somebody. Praise good work, regardless of who did it.

4. Be interested in others: their pursuits, their work, their homes and families. Make merry with those who rejoice; with those who weep, mourn. Let everyone you meet, however humble, feel that you regard him as a person of importance.

5. Be Cheerful. Don't burden or depress those around you by dwelling on your aches and pains and small disappointments. Remember, everyone is carrying some kind of burden.

6. Keep an open mind. Discuss but don't argue. It is a mark of a superior mind to be able to disagree without being disagreeable.

7. Let your virtues speak for themselves. Refuse to talk about the vices of others. Discourage gossip. It is a waste of valuable time and can be destructive and hurtful.

8. Take into consideration the feelings of others. Wit and humor at the expense of another is never worth the pain that may be inflicted.

9. Pay no attention to ill-natured remarks about you. Remember, the person who carried the message may not be the most accurate reporter in the world. Simply live so that nobody will believe him. Disordered nerves and bad digestion are a common cause of backbiting. Remember, man spreads the rumors but God has the records.

10. Don't be anxious about the credit due you. Do your best and be patient. Forget about yourself and let others "remember." Success is much sweeter that way.

# Chapter 3 The Pastor

## Preacher, Wait Your Turn

A national evangelist by the name of Manuel Scott, Jr. delivered a lecture to a group of preachers in which he simply shared the importance of waiting to Pastor if the pastorate is indeed in fact the ministry/office that God has called us to. I would have to say that I strongly agree with his statement that most Associate Ministers are in serious need of **guidelines** to help them assist their pastors.

### Are You Sure God Is Calling You to Be Pastor?
Due to the tremendous influence of black Baptist tradition, most preachers automatically assume that God is calling them to the Pastorate, when in fact, God may be calling them to another kind of ministry. For Preachers, please realize that today there are many, many kinds of viable ministries that you can have other than the Pastorate: Evangelism, Armed Services chaplaincies, Christian Education, Hospital/Prison ministries, Youth and Young Adult Ministries, Media Ministries, Teaching Ministries, Social Work Ministries, Suicide Prevention Ministries, Family and Marriage Counseling Ministries, to name a few. A lot of churches struggle when the man they affectionately call Pastor was not called to be a Pastor.

### Wait Your Turn
In light of what we have stated above, and if you are convinced that God is calling you to be a Pastor someday, then, seriously recognize that you must wait your turn. To be more simply put, as an Associate to your Pastor, you must patiently demonstrate consistent, helpful, and true allegiance to your Pastor, until God calls you to be a Pastor. *Galatians 6:9; 1 Corinthians 15:58; Romans 8:28; Isaiah 40:30-31; Psalm 40:1-3; Psalm 30:5*

**What Happens When You Do Not Wait Your Turn**
When you don't wait your turn, you anger God; frustrate and destroy yourself; and even worse, you give yourself a very poor name among other Pastors and Preachers. Failing to wait your turn puts you in risk of contaminating your spirit with jealousy, hatred and bitterness: a contamination that will follow you wherever you go. It will not do you any good to change your church, if you don't change your negative spirit first. The best way for God to elevate you (to the Pastorate or whatever) is for you to acquire a spirit of excellence as discussed earlier.

**Why Is It So Difficult For So Many Associate Ministers to Wait**
Some associates have an oversized ego—that is, they are so full of self-pride until they actually believe they can do a better job than their Pastor. Some Associates have an undersized sense of integrity (a preacher's togetherness based on their commitment to being honest, moral, dependable and loyal). Some Associates have an out-and-out distaste for Authority (any kind of Authority) – for some Associate Ministers, because they think they know everything, do not want the Pastor to tell them anything. Some are "glory and glamour" addicts to the point that they must always be in the limelight. Some have no concept whatsoever of the "pay-your-dues" principle—that is to say, many Associate Ministers do not have the foggiest notion of the cost Pastors have paid in order to lead their people. Some Associates, because they have listened to disgruntled church members, are foolish enough to believe that their Pastor is deliberately trying to hold them back.

**What Should You Do While Waiting Your Turn?**
1. Seriously come to terms with the biblical truth that God still gives churches Pastors; therefore, realize that your Pastor has been placed where he is by God himself.
2. Carefully observe the right and spiritual (therefore effective) things your Pastor does.
3. Learn how to praise and diplomatically defend your Pastor in public.

4.  Examine yourself in light of the qualifications of a Pastor as stipulated in 1 Timothy 3:1-7, and honestly determine where you fall short as a prospective Pastor.
5.  Keep your distance from church cliques, complainers, gossipers, and by all means, known enemies of the Pastor.
6.  Use the time that you have to get to know your Bible thoroughly.

## Church Leadership: Pastor or Preacher

Is there a difference between a pastor and a preacher? Many churches have great preachers, but pastoring is more than just preaching. There may be many similar characteristics between the two, but the Pastor's heart is very different.

All pastors should "study to show themselves approved" (2 Timothy 2:15), striving to be the best preacher they can be. However, the weekly service is only a small part of our ministry as pastors – there is much more to pastoring than preaching weekly church services.

Within the ministry gifts or offices, there are what many call the "fivefold" ministry. Paul listed them, "And he gave some as apostles, and some as prophets, and some as evangelists, and some as pastors and teachers" (Ephesians 4:11). They are as follows:

**Apostle.** An Apostle is a foundation layer or pioneer (1 Corinthians 3:10). They will usually flow in and out of all five offices or gifts.

**Prophet.** The Prophet speaks for God to the church, and are usually called to speak to the Church as a whole. This office is very different from the spirituals or manifestations spoken of in 1 Corinthians 12 and 14. Many within the body may be used by God to give a prophetic utterance and not hold the office of a Prophet.

**Evangelist**. Again, this is an office/gift given to the church. Evangelists are soul winners, but there may be many in the body of Christ who have a burden to win souls who do not hold this office. The Evangelist is called to stir up the Church – motivate and move its people into action.

**Pastor**. The Pastor is married to the church. He is committed to and his heart has been given to her.

**Teacher.** The Teacher's heart is for truth. Their desire is to dissect the Word to make sure the church and it's people thoroughly understand the truth of scripture.

### The Role of a Preacher
To preach literally means, "To proclaim after the manner of a herald". This always implies exhortation and "always with the suggestion of formality, gravity and an authority which must be listened to and obeyed". The Preacher has a passion for the Word of God and presenting the message God has given him for His people – the Church. All of the first four ministry or office gifts often function as a preacher, particularly the Prophet and Evangelist.

### Characteristics of a Pastor
The pastor will function as preacher when feeling a sense of urgency for his church and people, and when exhorting them to apply the truth he has taught. There are specific characteristics in the heart of a pastor that may not be prevalent in the other ministry or office gifts.

1. **Pastors must be able to teach.** The pastor is always a teacher. His heart is to teach and instruct his people. It has often been pointed out that in Ephesians 4:11, "He gave some ... as pastors and teachers", is one gift. There may be teachers given to the church that are not pastors, but a pastor is always a teacher.

2. **Pastors must feed the flock.** Peter said, "Feed the flock of God which is among you" (1 Peter 5:2). One of the Pastor's primary jobs is to feed his people the word. Where a teacher may have a specific thrust in his teaching, a pastor seeks to feed

his people a balanced diet of the Word. Paul as an Apostle, functioning often as a Pastor, said, "For I have not shunned to declare unto you all the counsel of God" (Acts 20:27). This is why a pastor will usually be an expositor of the Word and frequently teach through entire books of the Bible.

3. **Pastors must shepherd the flock.** The pastor is a shepherd. "Feed" in both Acts 20:27 and 1 Peter 5:2 can be translated as shepherd. Peter goes on to say, "Exercising oversight" (1 Peter 5:2). The pastor or shepherd is to be the primary overseer of the church and the elders under shepherds, with Jesus being the Chief Shepherd (1 Peter 5:4 and 2:25). The pastor is to exercise oversight over the body and all the ministries of the church, much of which may be delegated.

4. **Pastors must protect the flock from false teachers and doctrines.** Paul warned the Ephesian elders upon his departure, "Be on guard for yourselves and for all the flock, among which the Holy Spirit has made you overseers, to shepherd the church of God which He purchased with His own blood. I know that after my departure savage wolves will come in among you, not sparing the flock; and from among your own selves men will arise, speaking perverse things, to draw away the disciples after them" (Acts 20:28-30). Pastors are to protect his people from wolves (false teachers). This is why one of the pastor's primary jobs is to teach. His is to teach and equip his people with sound doctrine so they are ready when someone attempts to bring in false doctrine, "speaking perverse things."

Notice, "from among your own selves men will arise, speaking perverse things, to draw away the disciples after them" (Acts 20:30). There are often those from among the body that will arise to attempt to steal disciples out from under the pastor. It will often come in the form of, "What do you think about this?" "I'm not sure I agree with what the Pastor said here." "What do you think about the decision the leadership made?" It most generally begins with casting doubt in the people's heart concerning the pastor and/or leadership. This is where division usually begins in the body – the tongue (James 3:5-6).

This is where the pastor (shepherd) is to fight off the wolves. I believe this is what Paul was dealing with, at least in part, when he said, "Preach the word; be instant in season, out of season; reprove, rebuke, exhort with all long suffering and doctrine. For the time will come when they will not endure sound doctrine; but after their own lusts shall they heap to themselves teachers, having itching ears" (2 Timothy 4:2-3).

Division can often be dealt with on the congregational level before it ever gets to the pastor. When God's people are well equipped by a pastor's teaching and shepherding they can stop this type of divisiveness before any major damage is done. I believe this was what Paul was dealing with when he said, "Mark them which cause divisions and offences contrary to the doctrine which you have learned; and avoid them" (Romans 16:17).

When divisiveness begins, abruptly stop it. This is not the time to be gentle but swift – rebuke is needed to arrest it. We should say, "Stop it now. I don't want to hear any of that negative junk. That is my pastor, leader, elder. I love you, but I don't want to hear this type of divisiveness. Please, shut up!" This may seem harsh, but if this kind of action is taken right away many church splits can be avoided.

5.  **Pastors must go after stray sheep.** A pastor/shepherd goes after lost or stray sheep. Jesus dealt strongly with this in Luke 15. He illustrated it with three examples: lost sheep, coin and son. The pastor is to go after missing sheep. He is to search for, go after, and bring back into the fold those who have strayed from the fold. If a person has missed two to three weeks of church, something is apparently wrong. I realize the pastor may not be able to always do this himself, especially when a church has grown beyond a certain point, but he can make sure it is getting done. This is where delegation is need-

ed.  This can also apply to following up on visitors.  Get contact information for anyone who visits your church and make sure someone reaches out to them.  A letter or e-mail should be sent out to them the following day after they visit the church. Before the following Sunday, they should also be contacted by phone and/or receive a personal visit.  Many visitors (who could have been a wonderful addition to the church) are lost because they are not followed up on.

6.  **Pastors must spend time in prayer.**  It was Samuel who said, "Moreover as for me, God forbid that I should sin against the LORD in ceasing to pray to you: but I will teach you the good and the right way" (1 Samuel 12:23).  A Pastor has a constant burden to pray for his people, even when they are in rebellion.

7.  **Pastors must have vision.**  "Where there is no vision, the people perish" (Proverbs 29:18).  A pastor is constantly seeking vision for the church as to what God wants, and plans accordingly.  Some translations have "progressive vision".  The vision the pastor receives is continually unfolding.

8.  **Pastors must provide order and structure.**  Paul instructed a young pastor named Titus, "For this reason I left you in Crete, that you would set in order what remains and appoint elders in every city" (Titus 1:5).  "Set in order what remains" or what is lacking.  A pastor is constantly planning and seeking the Lord regarding how to organize and structure the church.  Structure is imperative for the success, prosperity, and growth of the church.  This is progressive.  As a church grows, it will need restructuring at every new stage of growth.  God can bring us new people, but if we do not structure for growth, we will not be able to maintain it.  A pastor must be an organizer.

**Are you a pastor or a preacher?**
Individual pastors may not always have expertise in every area mentioned, but they will at least see the need and have a burden for each of these aspects of pastoring.  Where a pastor may be lacking in a particular area, God will bring in someone who makes up where he lacks,

"ye are complete in him" (Colossians 2:10). It's important to lay ego aside and let them help when God brings them to you!


## The Pastor – His Identity and Authority

We have ceased to think theologically about the ministry. Instead, we characterize it almost exclusively in functional or institutional terms. There are at least two reasons for this shift in emphasis. On the one hand there are the new developments in clinical psychology and counseling procedures and on the other the requests of parishioners, the denominational programs, and the culture of the local community. Much has been written about various aspects of pastoral theology, but there is a remarkable scarcity of literature that explores the theological issues that lie behind it.

Much of modern pastoral psychology is abandonment to this American pragmatism. It is an aping of American scholarship as it demonstrates its pragmatic motivation. There seems to be a disdain for a careful study of the biblical view of the ministry.

Such is the minister's dilemma. He is faced on the one hand with the traditional biblical definitions (though often poorly developed and frequently caricatured) and on the other with the set of functional expectations by which his service is judged. In addition he is strongly influenced by the attractiveness of new developments in clinical psychology and counseling procedures. Therefore he faces basic ambiguities in performing his task.

The minister serving in today's secular culture is also confronted with an eroded image of the pastor. He is no longer the most educated man in the community or the one who elicits the mental image of a paragon of virtue. A recent poll showed that only eight percent of the population recommended the role of the clergyman as the preferred profession, far behind the doctor, engineer-builder.

How will the pastor establish or regain his identity? Is he the evangelist who goes house to house, attempting to gain conversation, the
friendly church visitor, or the counselor who deals with the people's
problems in his office?

Before we turn to an explicit delineation of the authority of the pastor-
teacher it should be pointed out that every Christian has a ministry.
Every Christian has an office, a mission to the world. It is, however,
misleading to say that every Christian is a minister. Rather, he has a
unique gift and is called to testify in his own calling by word and
deed. In a Reformed view of life and the world there are no secular
callings, but all vocations are to be performed for the glory of God
and under the direction of God's word.

Ephesians and the Pastoral Epistles make plain that the church has a
specialized ministry. Some men were set apart and given by the as-
cended Christ to the church for its edification. The pastor-teacher is
to serve the people of God in such a way that they are able to perform
their ministry. The people of God must see the minister as a gift of
God's grace in both his origin and service. And the pastor himself
must cultivate a sense of both dignity and deep humility because of
the office he bears.

The biblically mandated function that will give the pastor his sense of
identity is preaching. It becomes the foundation for all other functions. The pastor is the verbal agent, the instrumental spokesman for
God.

The past president of the American Academy of Homiletics in the pe-
riodical *Preaching Today* exhorts his readers to recognize that
preaching is indispensable for it is the transmission of the Word of
God. He then stresses, however, that all the questions concerning the
effectiveness of preaching signal its end as we know it.

Herein is the minister's identity and source of confidence. The au-
thority of the minister rests in Jesus own word (2 Peter 1:17-21),
"How then shall they call upon Him in whom they have not believed?
And how shall they believe on Him in whom they have not heard?

And how shall they hear without a preacher? And how shall they preach unless they are sent? Just as it is written. How beautiful are the feet of those who bring glad tidings!" (Rom. 10:14-15). So they are not scribes, not sycophants representing a mere human boss. They are heralds of the kingdom making a solemn declaration of forgiveness or judgment. There will be a real sense of mission on the part of the minister and a respect for the office by others if the authority is Christ's.

## Knowing Who You Are and What You Do Helps!

There's confusion today about who ministers are and what they do. A few years ago the Educational Testing Service conducted a study on ministerial identity. One thousand lay leaders in various denominations were asked to give adjectives and profile statements of what they considered to be an "outstanding minister." This information was then given to a group of psychological testers. The testers were not told who was being described. When asked to identify the person being described, they said, "A junior vice-president of Sears-Roebuck."

### Who Are You?
The problem of blurred identity can create difficulties as you begin a new pastorate. You must be sure within yourself of some basic truths about your identity. Three things must be firmly pegged down. First, you must be aware of your own personhood. Your humanity is undeniable. Failure to accept that you have needs, fears, weaknesses, and idiosyncrasies is to fail to accept reality. The denial of your humanity either by yourself or by others makes you subject to expectations that defy finiteness of ability, energy, and time. The fact is your abilities are limited and your available energy and time are not without end.

### Do You Have a First Name?
Because of your humanity, special care should be taken not to create or encourage unrealistic expectations for yourself. Determine to be the best pastor possible; attempting to be a superhuman pastor can

result in disappointment and disillusionment for yourself and others. Human inability to accomplish superhuman tasks can create an unnecessary sense of personal failure and guilt.

## Did Someone Call Your Name?

A second fact to peg down is that you are a called person. You are called of God. You share with all Christians the call to faith. Every believer has experienced and responded to the initiative of God's Spirit to accept Jesus Christ as Savior and Lord. But your calling has two additional dimensions. You have been called to ministry. This is the call to devote one's energies in some ministry of the church. This call probably came as an inner disturbance, questions about life's meaning and direction, a recognition of need, and a sense that God desired your life as an instrument of his work in the world. You have also experienced a corporate call. In the process of becoming the pastor of a local church, you have been interviewed, discussed, investigated, and "called" by the body. Clarity and personal certainty about your callings are essential to your ministry in your new church.

## Are You Somebody Important?

The third thing to peg down is that who you are and what you do has standing and significance among others. Ministry is not something people do who can't do anything worthwhile. Your work is of ultimate importance in the world. You are a professional person offering important services to the church and to persons. To be identified as a professional is not to minimize ministry or to take it out of the realm of God's calling. By simple definition ministry is a profession. James Glasse helps us see the minister as a professional person. Glasse provides five qualifications of a professional:

*He is an educated person.*
The professional is a person who is "master of some body of knowledge." The minister must be one who is well studied in a specific body of material. This would include Scripture, the history of the Christian faith, and the human condition and nature.

*He is "master of some specific cluster of skills.*
The minister is one called on to perform certain tasks. Whether it is preaching a sermon, making a hospital visit, or counseling a distressed person, he must be able to perform his work.

*He is an institutional person.*
The minister renders his service through a "historical social institution of which he is partly servant, partly master." The church is that institution.

*He is a responsible person.*
The minister "professes to be able to act competently in situations which require his services."

*He is a dedicated person.*
The minister is one who "professes' something, some value for society."

These recognitions call us to consider our work more highly than we otherwise might. They also help us face major questions in contemporary ministry:

> Who is the minister accountable to?
> To whom is he answerable for the proper performance of his work?

The following suggests the importance of a clear self-understanding and identity in the minds of others.

If the pastor is an employee, then he is accountable to …
> His "employer" –
> The local church,
> Its officers;
> Or denominational agency.

If the pastor is an independent professional, then he is accountable to
…

> Himself,
> His professional colleagues,
> Other ministers.

If the pastor is a person, called of God, then he is accountable to …
> God,
> Himself,
> His family,
> His colleagues,
> His church,
> His denomination.

Glasse concludes that the minister as professional is indeed an accountable person. His accountability grows out of his professionalism. The final, ultimate basis of the evaluation of his services is his dedication to the values of his profession.

## What's Your Job?
Just as you must know who you are, it is necessary to know the nature of your work. Pastoral ministry is a specific task. Rather, it is a set of tasks. These tasks are determined by the nature of ministry as described in Scripture and determined by the needs of the church.

## Is It Preacher, Counselor, or Administrator?
The Bible presents several images of the person of God. They suggest what he is about and what he does.

In the Old Testament there are three such images—prophet, priest, and king. The New Testament presents some similar images. In Ephesians 4:11, Paul mentions some of them. He says that God gave some to be apostles; some, prophets; some, evangelists; and some, pastors and teachers.

These Old and New Testament images are related in the similarity of the tasks performed. The prophets of the Old Testament declared

God's message. The prophet/evangelists of the New Testament were likewise the proclaimers of God's message.

The work of the priest in the Old Testament was the care and guidance of the people according to the dictates of God's law. They instructed the people in the law and called them to live their lives around its truth. Interestingly, this is the same function of the pastor/teacher of the New Testament.

The kings of the Old Testament were primarily concerned with giving oversight and direction to the national or corporate life of the people. Similarly apostles of the New Testament church were looked to by the church for corporate direction.

### Basic Functions
1.  Proclaim, Speak forth God's message
2.  Care, Counsel, and Guide in understanding and doing righteousness
3.  Lead, govern, provide direction to the corporate life of the people

Today the work of a pastor involves all three basic functions. Ernest Mosley in *Called to Joy* helps us see that the pastor's work encompasses the tasks of proclamation, care, and leadership.

The pastor stands before the people as one declaring the Word of God. He stands with them providing guidance, counsel, and care. He works among them providing leadership to the church's growth and mission. Mosley indicates that a pastor cannot devote himself solely or mainly to only one of these tasks. To perform his full responsibility, the pastor cannot depend on either the pulpit, the counseling chamber, or his position as congregational leader alone. There should be a strong degree of equality of each of these.

Each task is equal in importance. They are interlocked to form a whole. They interrelated and interdependent, to the extent that a pastor excludes one function or minimizes it, he diminishes his effectiveness in other areas. If he does not recognize and perform his care task, he harms his effectiveness in proclamation and leadership. If he does not accept responsibility for his leadership task, he undercuts his effectiveness in proclaiming the gospel and caring for people. It is crucial therefore that you recognize the importance of each area of work as a pastor.

## Is It Pastor?

Pastoral ministry is necessary for the health and productivity of the church. It exists for the church. The church does not exist to support the pastoral ministry. This distinction is necessary for a clearer understanding of the relationship between the church and the pastor's ministry.

There are two different and conflicting understandings of the place and role of the pastor in the church. One view suggests that the pastor, and particularly his ministry, is the focus of the church's life and effort. It says that the church's leadership and general membership find their purpose in providing help and giving support to the pastor's ministry. In effect this view implies that the church exists for the pastor's ministry.

The second understanding suggests that the pastor's ministry is for the church. It says that the church is the object of the pastor's ministry rather than the supporter of his ministry. This is not to say, however, that the pastor as a person does not also receive personal encouragement and support as a member of the church. He also needs ministry. But his role as pastor is a supportive and enabling task.

This second pattern is apparently what Paul had in mind in his description of the work of the ministers in the church. In Ephesians 4:11-12 Paul indicated the purpose of their ministry—perfecting of the saints, for the work of the ministry, for the edifying of the body of Christ.

According to this passage, every form of ministry finds its purpose in the development of the church for ministry. Some persons resist and others reject this approach to ministry. They oppose the idea that the pastor is in a secondary, less than primary position. Yet Jesus himself describes ministry as servant hood. The role of minister is servant. Jesus taught that the measurement of greatness and significance in his kingdom was different from that in the world.

We have come then to two major principles in pastoral ministry. First, pastoral ministry involves a balanced approach to proclamation, care, and leadership. Second, pastoral ministry involves a servant role to help the church grow toward maturity and engage in ministry. With these two facts clearly in mind we need to consider the phases of a pastor's ministry in a church.

## The Pastor Holding His Own Attention

The pastor must completely lose himself in the truth he is preaching. One of the most important things for any Christian to do is lose himself. The best sermons that are preached are those in which the preacher loses himself in the truth that he is delivering. Hence, it becomes vital for the pastor to capture his own attention. The pastor must capture himself; the truth must hold him hostage. He should not be aware of how well he is preaching, how he looks, the opinions that others hold of him, etc. There are times that he should not even know where he is or be conscious that he exists. He is totally lost, not in the delivering of a sermon, but in the delivering of his soul!

The pastor must keep his mind on one thing and one thing only He has people who need him, and he has a truth that will alleviate their needs. He has people who are weak, and he has a truth that is strengthening. He has people who have fallen, and he has a truth that will lift them. He has people that are sad, and he has a truth that will cheer them. He has people who are bereaved, and he has a truth that will comfort them. His total mental occupation should be on the one thing of administering to his people the thing that will satisfy their needs and their hungers.

The pastor must not let anything or anybody steal the control of his mind or make him to follow their thinking. It is important that the pastor who has found the message for the hour not allow his mind to be controlled by anything else until that message is preached! He must not allow external stimuli to capture his thinking and take it off of the delivery of his soul through the truth that God has given him with which to meet the needs of his people.

The pastor should do his heavy praying earlier and not right before the service. Even such a thing as feeling his need of power can get his mind off of the truth he is about to deliver. Please do not misunderstand me. I believe that every man of God should spend seasons with God. He should walk with God. He should often pray throughout the night, and the rising of the sun should find his cheeks stained with tears. I do, however, believe that the best time for such praying is before and during the preparation of a message. When one has found the message and is waiting to deliver it, he should not be thinking about power for himself but rather meeting the needs of others. Before the message his mind should be totally on his people and their needs.

The pastor should go to church early and relaxed. His sole desire should be to feed his people what they need for their spiritual growth and health. He may go to his study early and think of his people as they are now preparing to come to church- they are bathing, dressing, getting in their cars and driving. They are coming to hear God's man give them what they need. In a relaxed atmosphere he must think of them and love them with his mind always fixed on the truth that God has given him for his people for that day.

The pastor should not allow any friction to exist at home. It is now Sunday morning. Nothing must take his mind off of the surgery he is about to perform. If someone at home starts dealing with something negative, he should deftly avoid it. If there is ever a time when a preacher should agree with his adversary, it is on Sunday morning and Sunday afternoon before he ministers to his people and their needs.

The pastor should not be with anyone over five minutes at a time on Sunday morning. A lengthy conversation can be used to capture the mind of God's man and to get it off of the truth that God has given him to deliver. This does not mean that the pastor should be aloof or sharp; it simply means that he should guard himself to see that he controls his mind before preaching. There is nothing the Devil would rather do than get the pastor's mind off the truth. The Devil does not want God's people to be healthy; he wants to dilute the medicine, to pervert the diagnosis and to prevent the cure. He often uses good things as substitutes for the best in achieving his goal.

The wise pastor will not mingle with the crowd for any length of time before preaching. Negatives may be mentioned that could discourage him. Heavy thoughts could be used as a cloud to cover the truth that he must deliver to those whom God has made him the under-shepherd.

The pastor should not think or talk business matters within two hours of preaching. The pastor is unwise who has committee meetings or deacons' meetings before services. Dealing with business matters could be used of the Devil to divide the mind of the Pastor.

The pastor should not counsel before the service. At times I may counsel after service but never before. This could divert my attention from what God wants me to say and give to my people. This is another way that my mind can be captured and directed away from the truth of the hour.

The pastor should not read notes or mail before the service. The worst of these could destroy his spirit, and the best of these could capture his mind. Every Sunday I get dozens of notes and letters, but I never read one before the service. I do not want a burden, a problem, a dissension or a complaint to capture my mind and take it away from the message that I am to deliver from God to my people.

The pastor should not read notes placed on the platform or pulpit. The pastor should not check the Sunday School attendance before the service unless he knows for a fact that it is a good one. If the attendance is noticeably down, it could bring the Pastor noticeably down and could divide his mind as he takes God's message from God's Word to God's people.

The pastor should not listen to anything negative on Sunday morning or within two hours of the Sunday evening service. Sunday is no time for the solving of petty problems or for listening to petty complaints. It is a time for God's man to be absorbed in his people and their needs and in the filling of their needs as God has directed him. No surgeon should go to the operating room with more dedication. No Supreme Court justice should go to his bench with more dedication. This is the highest hour in the life of a human being, when the living God has given to mortal man a message for His people. No responsibility is its equal. No burden carries its weight. No duty deserves more diligence and no heart deserves more devotion than that day chosen by God when that man chosen by God brings that message by God to God's people in order to meet their needs.

The pastor should not have a schedule that includes late preparation of his sermons. The pressure could be used by Satan. He should not feel that he has a deadline to meet.

The pastor should not wear clothing that would divert his attention. For example, I never wear a new suit on a Sunday morning or a Sunday night. If I have a new suit, I always wear it the first time to a preaching engagement out of town or where the people will not know it is new and where I will not be self-conscious. I do not wear a new pair of shoes to my own pulpit first. I wear them likewise while speaking out of town so that the people will not know they are new and so that I will be self-conscious. I must not have my mind on how I look or upon a garment that I am wearing. I must be totally lost in delivering the message from God to his people.

The pastor should not develop any ritual on Sunday that depends on others. His Sunday praying should be alone. I know a pastor whose entire day was ruined because he had a Sunday morning prayer meeting with his laymen and very few showed up. He was so discouraged that he did not deliver the message that God had given him, but rather chose the 11:00 hour as a time to use the pulpit for a whipping post, and the hungry sheep went unfed!

The pastor should not eat before preaching. On occasion I have eaten, and on such occasions, I have been aware that I was too full and my mind was taken from my message somewhat because of my discomfort.

The pastor should have self-control rituals before preaching. The pastor should choose a last thought before walking in the pulpit. As I walk in the door of the sanctuary at every service I think of one thought- that this could be my last sermon. I always ask God to help me preach as I would preach if I knew it was!

The preacher should remember before preaching how badly he wanted to preach before he ever got the opportunity. He should remind himself that this is that to which he looked, for which he longed and of which he dreamed. Now he is God's man, preaching to God's people God's message from God's Word in God's power.

The preacher should remember that someday it will end. The pastor should not judge the song service while it is in progress. This too can capture his mind and divert it from the message he is about to deliver. He should not allow himself to critique the song leader or the singing. He should not get up and try to improve the song service. Receive its blessings. Do not indulge in criticism on an ineffective song leader, or an ineffective song service could be used to capture the mind of the preacher. In principle he would be right, but he would not be prepared to stand in the place of Christ Himself and deliver the message that Christ would preach were He present.

The wise pastor will not choose a song leader who preaches sermons or gives devotionals between stanzas of the songs. Such palaver could steal a pastor's mind from God's message for the hour and capture his thoughts. If such a song leader is already employed, the pastor should not allow himself to think negative thoughts about him while he is rambling. Pastor, keep your mind on your sermon. Think of the needs of your people. Do not let your mind be captured.

The pastor should not appraise himself while he is preaching. It matters not how good the sermon is. It matters not how well the pastor is doing.  All that matters is that there are needy people.  The pastor knows their need and has the medicine that can heal them.  If the doctor makes a grammatical mistake while he is administering the medicine, it will not harm the patient.  It would be better if the grammatical mistake was not made, but the important thing is the patient and the cure.

The pastor should make his own announcements in the service.  Once again he is controlling his own mind and his own thoughts.  If someone else makes several lengthy announcements, the pastor's mind could follow him and detour from the mental path that God has chosen for him to travel that day.

The pastor should not give public responsibility in the service to others who would capture his mind from the truth he is about to deliver and from the people to whom he is about to deliver it.  A godly associate may read the Scripture, another godly co-laborer can lead the prayer; but this should not be a time for fellow-workers to rise and shine to tell their favorite little joke or preach their favorite little sermonette.

The pastor should not try to create a spirit in the service.  His mind should not be on the spirit of the service.  His mind should be on his people and the spiritual medicine he is about to administer to them.  That will take care of the spirit of the service.  Sometimes God's men are so busy in the early part of the services trying to create a spirit that they completely lose concentration.  Let God create the spirit.  The preacher should carry the burden and deliver the message given by God Almighty to His people through His messenger.

The preacher should not try to salvage a service.  For that matter, he should not even be aware that it needs salvaging.  He can destroy the purpose for the entire service by analyzing it, salvaging it, measuring it and weighing it.  The important thing about the service is the sermon.  If the preacher is alive, the service will come alive.  If the preacher is spiritual, the service will become spiritual.  If the preacher is totally lost in his ministry of representing his Saviour, the people will soon become lost in the spirit.

I think it is unwise to have testimonies before a sermon. I love testimonies, but the best time to have them is after the sermon. Even a testimony can capture the people's minds and capture the preacher's mind so that he will not control his own destiny and that of the service. This is not to minimize testimonies; they are very important and vital, but at preaching time they can become a competition with the message of the hour and with the responsibility of the messenger.

The preacher should have mental pictures of Bible events and Bible stories. This is one of the best ways to become lost in a sermon. For example, I have in my own mind a file of images of every story I know in the Bible. I can tell you what the prodigal son's house looked like. I can tell you how big his father was and what his brother looked like. I can tell you what Jacob looked like. I can describe Esau to you. I can tell you what Bethel was like. Such a mental file will help the pastor lose himself in his message, for he becomes actually a participant in the Bible story and a witness of all that is happening. He is then not just relating a story he has heard, but he is telling a story that he has seen.

The pastor should have a list of things that can get his own attention back. Sometimes in a service things happen that compete for the pastor's attention. Perhaps someone is moving, a baby is crying, or some other circumstance has entered the service. The pastor should know and have a list of those things that affect him enough to recapture him for his sermon. I have at least a dozen things that always warm my heart. It matters not where I am or who is present or what the circumstances are. To think of them is to inspire me. When I feel in a sermon that something has stolen me from my message, I use one of these things with which to recapture myself so that it can deliver me again to my mission of the hour.

The pastor should turn away from interruptions if they are being solved. For example, if a crying baby is being taken from the service, a pastor should look to the other side of the sanctuary and preach. The interruption will soon be over. He should not allow himself to witness it while it is in progress.

He should correct those interruptions that appear to be there to stay. For example, if there is a crying baby in the service whose mother is making no effort to remove him, it may hurt the service more to allow the child to stay in the sanctuary than courteously to ask the mother take the baby to the nursery or to the hallway. It is obvious that this problem is not temporary but that it is going to continue to disturb the service. The best thing for the pastor to do is face the problem, correct it and then use one of the aforementioned suggestions of things that always capture his attention to get his mind back on God's message for the hour.

The pastor should fall in love with his people. There are many ways this can be done, but one of them is to watch them during the service on the Lord's day. Look at the young people and realize the temptations that they face. Look at the older people and realize the anxieties that confront them daily. Look at the middle-aged people and realize the burdens and problems of life that are theirs. Spend some time on the platform loving your people. This will make you even more desirous to be to them what they need you to be and to give them what God has chosen for them to receive through His servant.

The pastor should decide whether or not the song being sung or the special being delivered will help him or hinder him in the delivering of his message and his soul. For example, there may be a song that is sung that is a bit peppier than the pastor needs to feel. Maybe a song has a beat to it that would not enhance the pastor's spirit that he needs to have as he preaches God's message. (I am not saying that the song would be one that is wrong to use, for this should never be done!) It may be a good song that is not exactly appropriate for the mental condition that the pastor needs to pursue.

The pastor should never preach to individuals. The very thought of an individual to whom he is preaching and/or scolding could steal his mind and capture it from the truth his people need to hear from him.

The pastor should never try to impress when he preaches. The purpose is not to impress; the purpose is to heal and to administer the cure.

The pastor should realize it is life or death! He is standing between the living and the dead as did Aaron of old. He is standing between Heaven and Hell. He is standing at the gates of eternity. Nothing is as important as that!

The pastor should preach for a certain result. If the pastor is to be successful in his mission, he must hold his own attention, and his entire focus on the day of his mission should be on that thing that God has called him to do. He is God's man with God's message from God's Word preaching to God's people in the power of God's Spirit, delivering to the people the very message that he feels that Jesus Himself would deliver were He standing before that very congregation.

# Chapter 4 The Pastorate

## 8 Pieces of Advice for a New Pastor

1. **Study the Scripture text you are going to preach on.** Read 2 commentaries on the passage. If you and the commentators agree, you are on the right track. Preach it!

2. **Take walks just for the purpose of praying**

3. **Learn everyone's name (first and last name) including the kids and janitor.** Make your own photo directory or flash cards if you need to.

4. **Schedule as many meals and coffees with people as possible.** Go to their workplaces and pick them up and take them to a place nearby that they often go when they go out to lunch. These meetings should be 45 minutes to 1 hour ½--no longer. Pay and turn in the receipts to the church. But only order very basic (as opposed to extravagant) things at the restaurants—equivalent to the price of a burger and soda. No dessert or alcohol on the church's bill. I'm tempted to say on this one, "It is better to ask forgiveness than permission" because I think you should do it even if the church does not typically pay for these sort of things. You will not get fired for meeting with lots of people. It is difficult to do it if you don't meet at restaurants and coffee shops in this day and age. People don't have time to go to your house and people often don't host people in their homes often. Every day meet with someone. Please! This is crucial.

Questions to ask when you meet with people:
Where did you grow up? Where are all the places you've lived? What is your job? Can you tell me enough about it so I really understand what you do? Is it terrible or great or just so-so? Why? How is your relationship with your boss?

What is your church background?  Why did you come to our church?

Should I just lift up these things we have already talked about to the Lord or is there something else I can pray about as well?  (In other words, you will know enough already to be able to pray for them). Do a quick prayer for them.

People will be surprised at how pleasant and interesting and good it is to meet the pastor and you will be relieved not to get into all the church politics until you get to know the people.  This person is more important than their complaint about the church.  When you get to know people, you will understand where they are coming from.  The person who is passionate about missions grew up in Africa.  The person who is passionate about pastoral care, works in a nursing home.  They are passionate for legitimate reasons!

As you can see from my questions, I would urge you to have low expectations for those first 1on1 meetings.  The point is to get to know people.  You will get close to some of them eventually.  You will need to have difficult conversations with some of them eventually.  But at this point, just enjoy people and get to know the basics.  This is critically important to eventually ministering deeply to them.

Pastoring is 1/3 preaching (study, prep, reading), 1/3 administration (meetings, email, phone calls, mail, chaos), and 1/3 pastoral care (meeting with people).  But you will have to initiate and be intentional to meet with anyone.  Very few will reach out to you.

5. **Read books by pastors for some sympathy.**

6. **Eventually, read some leadership books to help you analyze the organization.**  I am sure someone has told you that you shouldn't change anything when you to a new church for at least a year.  Well, forget it!  Don't change anything in a new church unless you are convinced that it needs changing!  Change anything you think that needs changing and anything you think you can

change without the laity killing you. Lots of churches are filled with laity who are languishing there, desperate for a pastor to go ahead and change something for the better. Lots of times we pastors blame our cowardice, or our lack of vision, on the laity, saying that we want to change something, but we can't because of the laity. We ought to just go ahead and change something and then see what the consequences are.

7. **Get 8 hours of sleep.** Get to bed the same time every night and get up the same time. You will thus have more resources of patience to keep your cool as you encounter all kinds of craziness, dysfunction, and beauty. The sleep will help you from getting too discouraged. Expect the organization to be terrible! Expect the people to be great . . . . once you get to know them.

8. **Learn the history of the church.** You need to be able to tell the old, old stories as well as anyone.

## Understanding the Ins and Outs of a Pastorate

**Sequence of Three Stages**
A pastor's ministry in a local church has three distinct stages. They fall in a natural sequence. Each stage influences each subsequent stage. This figure illustrates these stages:

1. Getting Underway
   Start-up is the first stage. It is the period the pastor gets his work underway in a new pastorate. Many crucial events occur during the start-up. First contacts and experiences between pastor and people take place then. The kind of relationship they will eventually have with each other begins to be formed here. It is during start-up that the so-called "honeymoon" period is experienced. This is followed by a time of "testings" which begins with the first hint of problem in the pastor-people relationship.

2. Maturing Relationships

The second sage of a pastor's ministry in a church is the "established ministry" stage. This period begins when the pastor and church come to a new maturity in their relationship. The relationship in this time is characterized by realities more than fantasies about each other. An effective start-up period enhances the established ministry stage. Unfortunately, many pastors never realize the potential of this second phase. This is because the established ministry stage is either abbreviated or aborted by a poor start-up.

3. Ending Positively

The third and final stage of a pastor's ministry in a church is called closure. This is the winding down or ending period. It lasts from a few days to a few months. Closure can be a healthy experience for both a pastor and a congregation. It can also be a destructive time. How closure is handled influences the next start-up stage both for the minister and for the church.

The pattern suggested by the second figure is potentially destructive to both the church and the pastor. If the ministry phases are prematurely ended or aborted by a poor start-up, the church and the pastor are robbed of their most fruitful time together. There is evidence to indicate, however, that this is a prevailing pattern. Among Southern Baptists the present average tenure of a pastor in a local church is approximately two years. Since the start-up phase generally requires from twelve to twenty-four months, the average pastor seldom moves significantly beyond the first stage. Actually, what often happens is that the average pastor will move through start-up to the point of the first problem. This is the point of transition from the first, start-up phase to the second, established ministry stage.

When the problem is confronted and realities about the church encountered, the pastor may decide to move to another church. It may also be true that the church does not know how to handle this struggle well; and instead of being committed to working through it with the new pastor, it seeks to force change. The result of either of these responses from the pastor or the church brings an end to the pastor-church relationship. This means that both the pastor and the church are faced with beginning another start-up with another partner without the benefit of a positive experience in the Last ministry. Too often the minister chooses a new ministry in a new church to avoid the pain of growing into the established ministry phase. Obviously the startup phase is critically important to both pastors and churches.

## Importance of a Good Beginning

In getting started in a church, a pastor must be aware of the crucial importance of the time of beginning. Some things that appear to be only details can turn into problems that retard the process and hurt the progress toward the established ministry stage. Some of these details have to do with the basic understandings you have with the church on the terms of your call to pastor.

When you are negotiating with a church, the following checklist may prove helpful in clarifying the contract. Even if you have already moved to your new church, check this list for anything that was not made clear. You will want to use it as a personal guide to questions to settle while negotiating with a church. You may want to suggest to the church that those matters left unresolved should be settled now to avoid misunderstandings later on.

## Checklist for Clarity in a Call

1. Church moves/provides moving expenses?    YES [ ]   NO [ ]
2. Church provides housing for pastor, family?   YES [ ]   NO [ ]
    If yes, in what form?
    Parsonage
    Allowance
    If allowance, how much monthly? $_____

3. Church provides utilities or allowance?    YES [ ]   NO [ ]
    If yes, amount: $_____
    Electricity         $_____
    Phone           $_____

71

| Water | $ _____ |
|-------|------------|
| Other | $ _____ |

4. Church assists pastor in purchasing home?   YES [ ]    NO [ ]
   If yes, indicate the following:
   Provides down payment as gift or loan in the amount of
   $_____ at an interest rate of _____% to be repaid at $
   monthly.
   Amount to be paid in full within _____ days of termination as
   pastor.

5. Monthly salary to begin $_____ with review for increase at the
   end of: Months _____ (How often?_____) Year _____
   Recommendation for increase to be made by
   _____ committee.

6. Monthly car allowance provided?          YES [ ]   NO [ ]
   If yes, in the amount of $_____ per month and _____ cents
   per mile for distant travel on church business.

7. Church provides insurance coverage?    YES [ ]        NO [ ]
   If yes, how much?
   > Health      $_____
   > Life        $_____
   > Retirement  $_____

8. Church provides annual book allowance?    YES [ ]   NO [ ]
   > If yes, annual amount $_____

9. Church provides weekly days off?          YES [ ]   NO [ ]
   > If yes, number of days _____

10. Church provides annual, paid vacation?    YES [ ]   NO [ ]
    If yes, number of weeks ___ first year; second year and thereafter

    ____

11. Is pulpit supply paid by church for vacation absences?
    YES [ ] NO [ ]

12. Church provides time off for:

    Revivals?           YES [ ]      NO [ ]    How much? _____
    State Convention? YES [ ]     NO [ ]
    National Convention?   YES [ ]     NO [ ]

13. Is pulpit supply paid by church for these absences?
    YES [ ] NO [ ]

14. Are expenses paid to conventions?     YES [ ]    NO [ ]
    Wife included?     YES [ ]    NO [ ]

15. Church provides time off for bereavement?  YES [ ] NO [ ]
    If yes, how much time? _____

16. Church provides time off for illness?     YES [ ] NO [ ]
    If yes, amount of time annually_____

17. Are salary and benefits paid during time of illness?
    YES [ ] NO [ ]    For how long? _____

18. Supply minister paid by church?     YES [ ]    NO [ ]
    For how long? _____

19. Church provides annual physical examination for pastor?
    YES [ ]    NO [ ]

20. Pastor is designated as supervisor of other staff? YES [ ] NO [ ]
    If no, who is designated and for which staff members?

21. Time off is provided for study leave and training conferences?
    YES [ ]    NO [ ]
    If yes, how much time annually? _____

22. Does church pay cost of job-related training?  YES [ ] NO [ ]
    If yes, how much of total cost? _____

**Clarifying Details**
These considerations and others need clarification. Since in most cases negotiations occur between a pastor selection committee and a prospective pastor, a free flow of information should take place. The congregation should be informed about the terms of the pastoral call and give its approval. These terms should be recorded in the minutes or in a letter since memory fades and leadership changes in the course of years.

Care to details in the start-up phase will reduce the possibility of misunderstandings later. Oversights and assumptions can become hurtful problems. Potential problems should be avoided. To do this, we need to consider some of the characteristics and problems of the start-up stage. The following explores some of the challenges a pastor confronts following the "honeymoon period."


## Passing the Entrance Requirements


During the start-up phase you can expect to face two different types of experiences. One is fun. The other may not be. The fun time is the period called the honeymoon. It's characterized by a lack of problems. It's a time of romance between yourself and the church. But the good cooperation and the almost unqualified positive feelings will finally be interrupted by the first shadow of problems.

**Surviving the Honeymoon**
Let's look briefly at the honeymoon period. There is no specific time period for it. The honeymoon may end before you are aware that it's over. Generally, you may expect it to last for the first four to twelve weeks of a new pastorate.

During this time a couple of things tend to happen. First, you and the church will likely idealize each other. Human frailties may not be apparent. This time of idealizing lasts from two to four weeks. After that an awareness develops that neither party is really perfect as first hoped. However, neither you nor the church is likely to admit this out loud. Because of an unwillingness to admit reality, an illusion is created based on denial. There is reluctance to give candid feedback to each other. The danger is not that feedback will occur but that, for fear of hurting each other's feelings, feedback is not given or received. It is easy to develop a false sense of security as a result of this. You may tend to operate with the assumption that people totally approve your actions. They may in fact be skeptical. You can easily mistake their silence for approval. In this atmosphere of non-communication, you may take directions and use methods inappropriate for the church.

Your own eagerness to succeed in the new church may further compound the problem. You may be afraid to see and hear the signals from people that say, "slow down," "not that way," "not at this time." The danger is that some mistakes of great substance may be made during this time. Wisdom says move slowly during these first few weeks and months.

## Challenging Your Credentials
The honeymoon period ends as you and the people begin to share your deeper feelings. Criticism may come. You may want to avoid hearing it, but it is best to hear and heed. Church members may lack the ability to share their feelings in a positive way. Both you and the church may be uncomfortable during this time. However, the end of the honeymoon marks the beginning of a potentially more mature relationship. Just as in marriage, the deepest and best experiences come after the first blush of romance. Likewise the first skirmishes in a church can become bridges of lasting and meaningful relationships.

The honeymoon may end with a soft murmur or a loud confrontation. If you are aware of the need to listen and be open rather than to withdraw and be defensive, this period can be a time of growth. The more you resist the words and feelings of others, the more powerful and emotional this period will become. Seeking feedback says to people that you care about their thoughts and feelings. This open, approachable style is far better than one that is closed, inflexible, and defensive.

## Testing Your Authenticity

Simultaneous to the honeymoon, another experience can be expected during the start-up period. This is the process of testing. It has to do with your own authenticity as a person and a minister. John Fletcher of the Inter/Met Project in Washington, D.C. coordinated a study of the problems church members have with ministers. In this study the major problems that were identified had to do with what was termed "religious inauthenticity." In describing the problems, lay persons said of ministers: "He speaks down to us ... did not have head and heart together..., pious...hypocritical..., lost on a mountaintop..., did not live the gospel in his own life...treated the congregation like children ... could not relate religion to life's problems."

During start-up the church may test your authenticity. They may watch for signals as to who you actually are as a person and as a minister. They may watch to determine consistency of words, actions, and spirit. The process of authentication testing touches three major levels. First, there is testing for your personal strength; second, there is testing for your professional ability; and third, there is testing of your sense of fairness and trust.

## Testing Personal Strengths

During the testing for personal strength, you may be challenged in your role as pastor of the church. Your pastoral authority may be questioned. The church may ask, "Can this man really become pastor here?" You may feel confused when this occurs. It is your assumption that you *are* pastor and that you automatically have the authority of your position. In fact, however, pastoral authority has to be granted to you by the church itself. You are not pastor simply because the church has asked you to be. YOU must *become* pastor. Before you do this, you may be challenged on issues dealing with power, authority, and purpose.

There is danger here of reacting to overcome the challenge by displaying an inappropriate spirit. If so, you may prove your personal strength but invalidate your authenticity as a minister. Another danger is that you may not act to meet the challenge and by your inactivity fail to validate the fact that you have the personal strength to be pastor. You can expect the testing through either overt actions to restrict your efforts or as covert behavior with persons refusing to respond to your direction.

The crisis surrounding this first level of testing your personal strength is actually the events that bring the honeymoon period to an end. Up to this point you may have assumed that you were being heard and followed. It comes as a surprise to realize this is not the case. Whether you can appropriately engage this situation, face it with love, and move the congregation with you through it are the issues.

**Testing Professional Skills**
The second level of testing relates to your professional authenticity. People do not receive your ministry to them just because you are the pastor of the church to which they belong. They discern for themselves that your own faith is real that you do have real abilities as a minister. Then they become willing to trust themselves, their hurts, and their joys to your confidence. This partially accounts for people turning to ministers other than their own pastors in time of need.

In discussing why they welcome a deeper relationship with one minister and not another, lay persons gave the following comments:

"I never expected any help from Rev, _____ because he needed more help than I did."

Comments about another minister paint a different picture:

"He had lived a full life and understood what I was going through.... He was a man of God and a man of the world."

"He knew what to do when he visited my mother. ... He would talk with her about her past, her teaching, and what she wanted in life.... He was not afraid of death like the others and like the doctors. She died a peaceful death and a lot of it was because ____ was able to be with her so much."

"He is so open…, and not embarrassed to express his feelings in public. I knew that I could talk with him."

Only gradually will the congregation accept you at deeper levels of relationship for ministry.

But you must be tested before you will be received at these deeper levels. Usually your first calls for help will come from the most distressed and dependent persons in the church. You may in fact find an inordinate amount of time spent with these people. It is possible, however, that this is exactly how the church will determine if you are approachable. Will you take time for people? Do you care? You will answer these questions as you minister to those who first trust you to be their minister. How you handle these persons who first come will say to others that you are the kind of pastor to whom they can go. Can you pass this test?

**Testing Fairness and Trust**
The third level of testing deals with whether you can trust others.
Can you share ministry with them?
Do you really trust the church to be a ministering body of Christ?
Do you want a mature relationship?
Do you want to make people dependent on you or to free them?
How will use the role of pastor?
Will you attempt to make persons, groups, and the church tools or partners?
Will you work to enable the church and its members to become co-workers in joint ministry? Until these questions are resolved, some persons will not commit themselves with you in ministry.

The process of testing actually goes beyond the start-up period. However, the initial impact of the testing experience is felt during start-up. How you weather the time of testing is a major factor in the movement from start-up to the established ministry period.

# Changing the Status Quo

"A new broom sweeps clean," says an old adage. You may assume that you are the "new broom" in your new church and try to "sweep the church clean." That is, to shape things up, make changes, get things moving. Start-up is often taken as the time to do that. You may feel a need to make all the changes you intend to make as early as possible.

## Hurrying Change

Changes attempted too quickly can create problems and hinder progress later on. One of the most common mistakes made by pastors during their first months in a new church is trying to make too many significant changes too quickly.

Caution should be used in making changes, especially within the first twelve months. This is especially true regarding changes in the worship services of the church. It is almost a standing practice of pastors to alter worship patterns in a new church. These changes are often attempted in the first two or three weeks. Keep in mind that change in the worship services is the most conspicuous and may be the most threatening to the church.

The worship service is the place most church members first encounter the new pastor. When changes are made in worship patterns, members may feel you are saying to them: "You did not know how to worship God until I came. Now that I am here, I will show you the right way." This may be both threatening and surprising to persons. As worship leader, you do have the authority to alter the services and to give appropriate direction. But along with this authority, you will need to exercise sensitivity. Consider the impact of the sudden change of having a new worship Leader who has his own ways of leading worship. Respect what the congregation is accustomed to. Remember the changes you make are likely those that design the service to what you prefer and not necessarily to the desires of church members.

Any changes ought to recognize the needs and feelings of others. Implement changes where they are clearly understood and wanted by the congregation. The type changes that are most effective during the first months are those that uplift morale, contribute to unity, and build hope. Actually, the best changes are additions to what already exists rather than deletions or substitutions.

Since there is danger in rapid and drastic change, how can you begin to shape the church? How can you begin to move the church in directions you feel are needed? Helping a church change requires some basic knowledge about how change happens with least resistance and greatest acceptance. The following concept of change will help you avoid making the mistake of seeking change too fast during start-up.

### Implementing Change
There are two basic and greatly differing approaches to implementing change.

### Using Your Position
First, you can use your position as pastor to make changes. By using your authority as pastor, you can persuade, announce, or even force change. This approach usually depends on coercive and manipulative actions. It can cause change to occur quickly and completely. However, it may cause anger and hostility. The emotions and actions it may trigger in others can be dangerous to the fellowship of the church. It can also weaken your effectiveness in other areas of your ministry. It is unwise to use this approach even though it appears to be a quick road to accomplishing your immediate objective.

### Using Your Influence
The second approach to changes involves the use of your personal influence rather than the power of your position as pastor. In this approach you seek to help people understand the need for change and develop positive feelings about it. Your influence continues as you urge them to try the new approach. As the church becomes willing to experiment with the new, you can encourage them to continue until they are thoroughly familiar with the new way. The church's comfort

and familiarity with an innovation determines whether it will be a permanent change or only temporary.

This approach to change is slower and depends on evolutionary rather than revolutionary development in events. The advantages are that the change will be more permanent and others will feel a commitment to it. Change that occurs in this way is not just your idea. It belongs to all who have had a part in causing it to happen.

The first approach is designed to use position power to bring about change. This approach depends on an almost blind acceptance by the group. Some, however, may resist and others may develop unfriendly attitudes to the change. The problem is that persons in the congregation do not have the same information you have or do not understand the situation as you do. It is better to share the information and help people interpret it. This concept is diagrammed in the second approach. Notice that personal influence is used in the communication of information. From this common information and understanding, common action can emerge. The ultimate goal is to lead the entire group to accept the information, develop positive attitudes, and implement the appropriate changes.


*Changes that should be made:*
1.


2.


3.


4.


5.

## Identifying Changes Needed

Use the following worksheet to identify the changes that are important for your church to make. Indicate why you feel the changes would be helpful. Think through them carefully. Ask yourself: Do these changes simply make things more familiar to me, or will they help the church have a more effective ministry? Will they build the fellowship of the church?

When you have identified the changes you want to make, the worksheet starting on page 63 can help you map your approach to causing the changes to occur. Remember, there are two different approaches: personal influence, which begins with helping people know why the change is needed; and position power, which seeks to make the change without concern for helping people understand and feel good about it.

Map your approach from the personal influence level up to the change you would ultimately like to see. Begin with step one, change in knowledge. Write in what people need to know to see the need for change. Then move to step two. What new attitudes will people need to have if the change is finally made? Then complete steps three and four.

## Charting a Course to Change

When you have completed the work sheet on a change, you will begin to see what you need to do to cause the change to occur. From step one you can see what you will need to teach or share with the people. From step two you can see what attitudes will need to be nurtured. Be aware that step one is easier to take than step two and that step two is easier than step three. The higher the step, the longer it will take also.

*What is the source and influence that indicated this need for change?*

## Expecting Unrealistic Results from Change

Your new church has some high expectations for your ministry. You have some visions too! The sense of expectancy is high. There is danger that both sets of expectations are unrealistic. The church may have confused the call of a pastor with the coming of a "savior." Many times the new pastor is seen as the answer to questions and the solution to problems. And you too may have an almost ideal image of the church. Apparently you saw some exciting qualities and opportunities in the church when you decided to become the pastor. However, as you begin a day-by-day ministry with the church and they begin to work with you, realities emerge.

### Inventory for Future Directions
It's important to develop a balanced perspective about your new ministry situation. You need to keep the beginning enthusiasm of seeing the church's qualities and opportunities. To ensure enthusiasm and optimism and to counteract disappointment and disillusionment, take an "assets and liabilities" inventory. Use the following "ledger sheet"

### Assets and Liabilities in My New Ministry Situation
1. The following qualities of the church impress me. (List some positive things about the church and your situation as pastor.)
   a. Positive factors about the church itself:

   b. Desirable qualities in individuals I have met:

   c. Things I like about the physical facilities:

   d. Impressions from staff/key leaders in the church lead me to feel that together we could have a good ministry here because:

   e. Terms of the call that I liked:

   f. Discoveries since I came that have excited or pleased me:

2. The following things do not please me about the church. (List those things that are liabilities. Be aware of things you did not deal with or ignored when you accepted the church as pastor.)
   a. Negative factors about the church:


   b. Undesirable qualities in persons I have met:
   c. Some disturbing feelings I have in talking with persons:


   d. Some limitations I see about the physical facilities:


   e. Impressions from staff/key leaders suggesting that we might have difficulties working together at these points:

   f. Terms of the call that were less than desirable:


   g. Surprises I have encountered that trouble me:


How do you feel about these assets and liabilities? Your feelings are important. They need to be recognized and dealt with in prayer and conversation. If you ignore or stifle your feelings, they can become destructive. There is a need to keep in touch with the feelings you have about the church liabilities. They can become dissatisfiers if you dwell on them. The romance you have for your new church and its attractive points can turn to disappointment unless you respond to liabilities in a mature manner.

One minister accepted a new church and soon after moving discovered that his new congregation had never done annual planning for its programs and ministries. In his first business meeting someone made a motion that the church have a revival. This motion was passed.

Another person made a motion that the new pastor serve as the evangelist for the meeting. The date was set for the revival in less than a month. This both angered and frightened the new pastor. However, instead of reacting in a negative manner, he used the experience to help the church leaders to see the need for long-range planning. By the fall of the next year, the church was presented with a calendar of activities and budget which reflected a year's plan for the church.

The realities are not the cause of discouragement. Rather the feelings you have about them are. If you feel the liabilities were hidden from you, then you may feel betrayed. If you see them only as problems, you may become critical. But if you see them as the realities of the situation, with counterparts in every church, then you can maintain a healthy attitude. Recognize that just as you have idealized the church, you have also been idealized. The fact is that the church is what it is and you are what you are. Efforts should be made to accept the congregation with both its strengths and weaknesses, its assets and liabilities.

## Establishing Ministry Relationships

The beginning question remains, Now that I'm here, what do I do? Your task is to design a specific plan of ministry in your new church. This plan will reflect major aspects of your work as well as some important actions you will need to take.

Your ministry in the new church will largely depend on the quality of your relationships with people. Good interpersonal relationships provide the channel for ministry. While you can minister to persons you do not know and who do not know you, this is not the kind of situation that holds the best potential for an effective pastoral ministry, especially among church members. You can build the kind of relation-that enable you to have a fruitful ministry. It's your responsibility to build these relationships. They are bridges between persons in the church and yourself as pastor. Without bridges there is a gulf.

**Taking Pastoral Initiative**

The pastor-people relationship has as its basic supporting beam your own initiative in moving toward persons. Just as you have to become pastor by establishing your authenticity, you must establish yourself as pastor in relationships to individuals, families, and groups in the church. This begins as you move toward them to identify with them as pastor. While it is possible to assume that the people will seek you as their minister, the initiative is not their responsibility. As pastor you need to begin your ministry by communicating, "I care, and I want to help you know that I am willing to identify with you."

**Through a Comprehensive Visitation**

One of the most appropriate ways for you to take pastoral initiative is through a comprehensive visitation of church members. You may want to visit every family personally. The purpose of this home visitation is to become personally acquainted with church members in the setting of their own homes. Wayne Oates has said that home visitation is the highest expression of pastoral care. Such visitation has been practiced by ministers throughout Christian history.

This visitation should not be done as a crash program to get into every home for a few minutes. It can be spread over a period of several months. Sufficient time should be spent with each family to accomplish the major purpose of the visit. After the initial visitation is concluded, it may prove helpful to continue a pattern of every-member visitation over a more extended period.

During these initial visits you will become aware of family members you might not meet otherwise. You can discern personal needs in the home and express your desire to be called on in times of need. You will also be able to gain an appreciation for the home situations of the persons who occupy the pews and Sunday School rooms on Sundays. Visits to church families are far more than social calls. They are pastoral calls. You are in their homes to express your interest and determination to be their pastor. You are there to discern the spiritual conditions of persons and to assure them of your care as their pastor. As you share with persons in home visits, you can sense their openness to Christian growth, opportunities for Christian service, and attitude toward the church body.

These home visits maybe either by appointment or on a drop-in basis. It is generally best to visit by appointment. There are two advantages to this approach. First, you will be committed to make the call. In this way good intention will not diminish into non action. Second, families can make the necessary arrangements for your call.

## By Identifying with Church Groups

Pastoral initiative is expressed not only in visits with church families but also as you identify with various groups in the church's life. A church is more than a collection of individuals. It is also people clustered in various groups. You can build relationships with these groups. By displaying an interest and investing time in the formal and informal gatherings of such groups, you can identify with them as pastor.

These groups include children and youth groups, Sunday School and Church Training classes, Woman's Missionary Union groups, Brotherhood, and any number of other clusterings of persons in the church. These groups can feel a sense of identification with you as Group pastor. It is not uncommon to hear persons in these groups comment to the group about "our pastor" or "our minister." These comments indicate a sense of personal closeness that grows out of identification. These identification comments are certainly better than those such as "the minister" or "that preacher" which indicate a lack of closeness. The difference in whether these groups have warm, close feelings or feelings of distance may depend on whether you have built relationships with them in their group settings. Use the following form and identify the specific groups in your church. Include in your list deacons, committees, and informal groups as well as those suggested above.

While pastoral initiative is the initial beam in the bridge to good relationships, it must be strengthened by other beams. One supporting beam is who and what you show yourself to be. This image is important to the process of building relationships.

**In Portraying a Genuine Image**
As you begin to relate to the people in the church, they will sense who you are as a person. Their discovery will either, enhance or weaken the relationship. It is important that you be a real person, that you are human. Often people feel that ministers are in a special category exalted above them. This may come from sensing a critical or judgmental attitude in the minister himself. Any pastoral behavior that causes persons to feel inferior will harm the ministry relationship. Also, any behavior that displays a self-righteous or judgmental spirit will cause people problems in relating to you. Beware of these possibilities in the pastor-people relationship and work to eliminate them.

A second support beam that can undergird your relationship with church members is your personal openness. An open, honest person is a person of integrity. When you allow persons to know you, two-way communication is made possible. They, in turn, will feel that they can be open with you and allow you to know them.

There is a risk in letting others know you. There are always those who want the pastor to be more than he can be. Some will want you to be above human weakness and temperament. As you relate to persons, you can deepen your ministry relationship by letting them know that you too are human. You have doubts, frustrations, and struggles in your own life. You do not have all the answers. If you present yourself only at the points of strength and success, many will be frightened or intimidated and will avoid relating to you. It is important to realize that people generally relate to others most at the points of common limitations and weaknesses rather than at the points of mutual strengths.

The third supporting beam in your relationship is your behavior. A pastor should display "incarnational behavior." It displays in flesh and blood the realities of the faith we profess. If we relate to persons out of love, it is incarnational. This means to display acceptance for them as who and what they are. It does not mean an acceptance based on conditions. An attitude of "I'll love you if..." is conditional love. It is important not to use your favor, friendship, or acceptance of persons to punish or reward them for behavior. Through the love relationship persons are challenged to live lives that are pleasing to God, but to manipulate them with an "if" in our love is unacceptable.

To be incarnational is to trust. Who are the people you are relating to in the church? They are Christians! They have experienced the grace of God. This must be your basic understanding of them. This means that you do not view them as reprobate sinners who must be watched with suspicion but as friends in the Lord who can be trusted. To relate to them in such a manner is bold behavior born of a kind of understanding worthy of a man called pastor. It is critical behavior in the development of the ministry relationship.

### Rules for Relationship Building
Below are some suggestions to aid you in developing your ministry relationships.

1. Help the other person open up by creating a climate of trust. One way to do this is to let the other person know what your relationship can contribute to each other.

2. Try to understand the other person's feelings. Communication is not only verbalization but also feeling what the other person is feeling at the moment and accepting him fully.

3. Be a good listener. Provide the other person the freedom to speak or express himself without projecting the feeling that you are prying for irrelevant information.

4. Try to be tactful. Don't be overly curious. Don't barge into private areas that persons obviously don't want to discuss.

5. Always respect the rights of others—what they feel, think, and express.

6. Be as nonjudgmental as possible where the person's value system may differ from yours.

7. Be honest with your feelings. People can usually tell if you are masking them; and when that happens, they will follow your example.

8. Never push a relationship. If you respect a person, you will always be considerate. Coming on too strong will often cause others to withdraw, especially if they have placed you on a pedestal. Allow the other person to move freely toward you if they are so inclined.

# Appendix 1 Standard of Leadership

**L**=Loyalty to the Pastor and his vision
**E**=Ethics
**A**=Accountability to the President and members of the Association
**D**=Dedication to the Association
**E**=Excellence
**R**=Respect the leadership
**S**=Spirit-filled and guided
**H**=Honor the calling first
**I**=Integrity to do the right thing when no one is watching
**P**=Passionate performance

# Appendix 2 The Christian's Creed

I am a Soldier for Christ! I am a warrior and one of God's anointed servants.

I serve God and God's people. I live the Christian Values.

I will always place God's will first. I will never accept defeat. I will never quit. I will never accept compromise. I will never leave a sinner behind.

I am disciplined, physically and mentally tough, trained and proficient in God's Holy Word.

I will always maintain my mind and my heart in God's unfailing love.

I stand ready to defend and to protect God's people and to take God's Holy Word to all of the people in the world.

I am a guardian of freedom and the Christian way of life.

I am a Soldier for Christ!

# Appendix 3 Decalogue for Supervisors

Moses' "ten words" are indelibly inscribed on the fabric of history. This Decalogue could possible help supervisors to be delivered "out of the house of slavery" (Ex. 20:2).

I.  *Thou shalt establish and maintain adequate communication.* The chief of staff is primarily responsible for making this "commandment" a reality. Every staff member has a share of this responsibility, but the major initiative is the responsibility of the supervisor.

    The implications of this command range from the giving of clear instructions by the supervisor to the feedback and suggestion flow from those supervised. There must be free and easily usable communications in all relational directions, or the communication is inadequate. The supervisor is the single most significant figure in making adequate communication a reality.

    Make it easy, even inviting, for workers to give feedback—their honest impressions, even about the supervisor's ideas. And don't miss getting the workers' suggestions, even the unusable ones. A worker whose unusable ideas are received will likely feel free to offer other ideas. Some of these might be good.

    Avoid the C-R-U-D syndrome—"Communication Restricted Unilaterally Downward." There must be ample freedom for workers to relate to persons anywhere in the organization for purposes of communication without suspicion or fear. The supervisor must have a very secure personality for adequate communication to be achieved.

II. *Thou shalt set clear and reasonable deadlines.* If deadlines are involved at all, they should be known by the worker at or near the beginning of an assignment. One way to help assure clear and reasonable deadlines is to ask the worker to suggest the time by which he thinks the assignment can be completed. If this time can be accepted by the supervisor, everyone is ahead.

Workers grow weary and sometimes resentful of unreal deadlines and of work assignments regularly imposed on too short notice. On the other hand, they usually feel more responsible for meeting deadlines they themselves help set.

III. *Thou shalt check appropriately on progress.* Ask workers how they are coming on work assignments. Avoid embarrassing workers. Be sure you don't nag by asking too soon or too frequently. Take care about asking in the presence of others. supervision can degenerate easily to "snoopervision." Give the leeway needed for workers to work effectively without feeling harassed.

Different workers need your interest at different intervals. Even the same worker might need your, "How are you doing on...?" more frequently on some assignments than on others. To learn to do this effectively, the supervisor must get to know his people and know generally what is involved in their work.

Sometimes you might need to keep a log of work assignments made, along with the progress at certain critical points, the time of expected completion, and the actual completion time. Such a log could help not only with operational supervision but also with worker development interviews and salary appraisals.

IV. *Thou shalt make needed help available.* Often when a supervisor asks, "How are you coming on...?" a worker reflects the need for help. Perhaps they need more time, more workers, more information or training, more material, different working conditions, different equipment, more money, less interference, more freedom, or any of a number of things.

The supervisor must assess the need, probably with the worker involved and possibly many others. if the need is valid and a solution can be advanced, the supervisor must see that the help is made available.

V. *Thou shalt encourage workers to seek help, responsibly.* Encourage workers to feel free to seek help when they have the need. Discourage their coming to you or seeking help on every little matter. The supervisor's door must be open, at least unlocked, so workers have access when they need help. When a worker has a problem, the supervisor has a problem, whether he knows it yet or not. Most often it is better to know and to support the worker in the situation.

VI. *Thou shalt develop solution-minded workers.* A supervisor's beatitude might be: "Blessed is the worker who suggests one or more possible solutions to every problem he brings." Usually there is a workable solution the problems encountered in a work situation. Help the worker feel responsible for finding possible options, not just locating or identifying obstacles. When a worker brings a problem to you, ask what he would suggest as a possible answer. Unless you have a significantly  better answer, accept the one suggested.

If a worker does not seem to have an answer, and if time permits, suggest he think further about it and come up with one or two suggestions. Set a time in your own thinking by which you will check with him to see if he has solved the problem. Or ask him to let you know when he has a possible solution. Commend him for good effort in finding answers. Acknowledge obstacles identified, but avoid commendation for mere identification of obstacles. Encourage the pursuit of solutions. He will soon get the idea.

You don't have to labor under the burden of feeling you must have answers to every problem. Your workers can become creative solvers of problems and can multiply productivity.

VII.　　*Thou shalt attack problems, not people.* You solve problems by attacking problems. In supervising you don't solve problems by attacking people. Attacking people almost always complicates the problem situation. It does not develop people, and it reduces productivity.

People need to be encouraged, not put down. Don't say, "Bert, I've told you numerous times that you need to,..." or "Bert, how many times must I tell you that...?" Rather, say, "Bert, I notice that there is still a problem regarding ... What do you suppose might be tried next?" or "What do you suppose might be an answer to this problem?" Direct the worker's energies toward solving the problem.

Avoid putting the worker on the defensive so that he consumes his best thinking energy protecting himself. For a normal person, survival is fundamental and becomes a primary concern when under personal attack. The worker under attack is at least partially a diminished person—you've cut away some part of him. And the problem is not solved either. Lay off!

VIII. *Thou shalt time guidance for optimum good.* Give guidance at the earliest appropriate time. If the task is such that you can risk letting the cycle of the situation run its full course, you might defer guidance until after the assignment is completed and offer it in a routine evaluation session. Sometimes, though, you must supervise early in a sequence of events in order to salvage a situation you can't afford to overlook.

Rarely should you deal with a worker on a sensitive problem while others are present. Wait, if you can, and handle it privately with the person involved. You might set a "wait limit," setting a time limit to allow the worker to recognize and to acknowledge the problem and to take the initiative to come for guidance. After the "wait limit" you must take the initiative. But remember the seventh "commandment."

IX. *Thou shalt avoid trivia.* Supervise. Give guidance on those matters which affect the success of the worker or of the work. This sometimes makes the work more interesting.

Discover those margins of error you can tolerate and still develop the workers and produce the work. Actively enter the situation when the margins of error are in jeopardy, or are actually exceeded. Overlook minor variations that don't cost too dearly. Evaluate the results, the end products, not every little indicator en route. Don't be "picky."

X. *Thou shalt learn from mistakes.* The lessons of experience should be instructive. Often the "tuition" we pay for these lessons is expensive. Why not get the message, and try to avoid making the same mistakes repeatedly?

Identify problems that occur again and again as you evaluate the work. Anticipate how you will avoid repeating mistakes. Develop policies and procedures to help you know in advance what you will do in repeated similar circumstances.

Try to lead your workers to suggest the policies and procedures they feel suit the situation. After all, if you are really a supervisor, your workers do the actual producing, not you. Your job is to produce the kind of setting and to give the kind of guidance that will enable them to become the persons they are capable of becoming, under God, and to do the work they are capable of doing.

# Appendix 4 Tips for Pastors and Christian Leaders

There are many little things in life of pastors and Christian Leaders that need to be given attention to. Some are listed below.

1. When entering the worship service and worship is going on, take a seat and do not go around shaking hands.

2. Do not enter another man pulpit without being invited.

3. Do you feel that a minister has to be seated in the pulpit to prove that he is a preacher?

4. We must learn to do what we are asked to do by the pastor or the one in charge.

5. Do not underestimate God's Churches. There are not big or small churches in God's eye. Do your best where you are and do not spend all your time looking for a larger church. God will promote you in due time.

6. Be careful how far you go to seek to pastor a church. After all, if God called you, He has an assignment for you. (Jeremiah. 1:5-10) also see the books of Jonah & Amos.

7. Being elected pastor does not say you are ready to pastor. You are able to pastor when you have been accepted as pastor.

8. Do not seek to know who voted for or against you. You are the pastor of all and must learn to love all.

9. Do not put all your trust in man; remember it is God who hired you. (Romans 8:28-31). (Moses and Israel)

10. Many pastors downfall is because of his wife's attitude, and allow the wife to pull the apron string.

11. Do not get the **BIG HEAD** because it seems that things are going **YOUR WAY**. (Luke 10:19-20)

12. Christ has promised you His Divine presence, if you obey His commands. (Matt. 28:19-20)
    A. Always remember His enabling Grace (Phil. 4:13, 19), (2 Cor. 8:9), (2 Cor. 12:9)
    B. The inseparable Christ (Romans 8:38-39)
    C. Believers are held close by His hand (John 10:28)

13. Remember God has promised that the gates of hell shall not prevail against the church (Matt. 16:18), (Acts 5:38-39). Peter was released from jail (Acts 12:5-11). Paul and Silas were released from jail (Acts 16:25-29).

14. It would be helpful if you would follow the Golden Rule.

15. You must be careful concerning your relationship with other ministers.

16. Be sure you understand that you will reap what you sow. (Gal. 6:7)

17. Remember we are our worst enemy. NO one can destroy me unless I permit him. Joseph's brethren hated him and sold him as a slave, yet it became a blessing for him and his brethren.

18. Remember that god is holding you responsible for what goes on in His name through the church. (Rev. 3:14-20)

19. Many pastors' problems stems from the fact that he at one time was a deacon. He gave the pastor a hard time and failed to support the program of the church. (Gal. 6:7)

20. Pastors should realize when he is officiating as pastor of the church; he is his wife's pastor and his children's pastor. They must be treated as any other member.

21. He should always know when he is pastor, husband and father.

22. Many pastors fail to work hard toward developing the congregation where they are, but always planning to leave for greater pastures. (I am reminded of a farmer that was asked why he did not plan a garden, or grow some chicken; his answer is I won't be here long and he died there.)

23. Many pastors spend most of their time looking for a gold mine; and another person comes and digs up the gold mine.

24. Make sure you treat all members the same. I know that some are better to you than others, but they are all your members.

25. You must learn to love all kinds of people; the good and the bad, for Jesus came not to call the righteous but sinners to repentance. The lost sheep became his most concern. (Luke 15:1-7).

26. You are now the shepherd, therefore you are to set the pace and lead the way.

27. You cannot pastor people if you talk out both sides of your mouth. You cannot agree with everybody but agree with what is right.

28. Be honest, truthful and trustworthy.

29. Remember in the church the majority is not always right. Remember the 12 spies that were sent to spy the promise land.

30. Respect the Pulpit, the Pastor and the People.

31. Always be prepared to preach and teach at all times.

32. Never ask your Pastor to preach or teach.

33. Be willing to assist the Pastor in whatever he needs.

34. Know the Pastor's Vision and the Church's Vision.

35. Never talk against your Pastor.

36. Be faithful in Sunday School, Bible Class and Worship Service.

37. Make sure your appearance is appearing.

# Bibliography

Blackaby, Henry T. and Richard Blackaby. *Spiritual Leadership: Moving People on to God's Agenda*. Nashville: Broadman & Holman Publishers, 2001.

Blizzard, Samuel W. *The Minister's Dillema*. 1956?

Bradshaw, Rickie L. *Transformational Leadership: Assumptions and Synopsis*. n.d.

Bryant, Charles V. *Rediscovering Our Spiritual Gifts*. Nashville, TN: Upper Room, 1998.

Buchanan, Edward A. *Developing Leadership Skills*. Nashville, Tenn.: Convention Press, 1978.

Burns, James MacGregor. *Leadership*. New York: Harper & Row, 1978.

Conger, Jay Alden. *The Charismatic Leader: Behind the Mystique of Exceptional Leadership*. San Francisco, CA: Jossey-Bass Publishers, 1989.

Copeland, K. Edward. *Riding in the Second Chariot*. Rockford, IL: PrayerCloset Publishing Company, 2004.

Drury, Sharon. *Handbook of Leadership Theory for Church Leaders*. n.d.

Dupree, Joseph D. *The Associate's Minister's Handbook*. Natchitoches, LA: First Baptist Church Amulet, 2004.

Engstrom, Ted W. *The Making of a Christian Leader*. Grand Rapids, MI: Zondervan Publishing House, 1976.

Fletcher, John C. *Religious Authenticity in the Clergy: Implications for Theological Education*. Washington, D.C.: The Alban Institute, 1979.

Glasse, James D. *Profession: Minister*. Nashville, Tenn.: Abingdon Press, 1968.

Greenleaf, Robert K. *The Servant as Leader*. Indianapolis, IN: Robert K. Greenleaf Center, 1991.

Gulledge, Jack. *Proclaim*. n.d.

Herrington, Jim, et al. *Leading Congregational Change: A Practical Guide for the Transformational Journey*. San Francisco, CA: Jossey-Bass Publishers, 2000.

Holmes, III, Urban T. *The Future Shape of Ministry: A Theological Projection*. New York: Seabury Press, 1971.

House, Robert J. *A 1976 Theory of Charismatic Leadership*. Toronto: University of Toronto, Faculty of Management Studies, 1976.

Hyles, Jack. *Teaching on Preaching*. Hammond, Ind.: Hyles-Anderson Publishers, 1986.

Jordan, Michael, Mark Vancil and Walter Looss. *Rare Air*. San Francisco: Collins Publishers, 1993.

Laub, James Alan. *Assessing the Servant Organization: Development of the Servant Organizational Leadership Assessment (SOLA) Instrument*. Florida Atlantic University, 1999. Thesis/dissertation.

Maxwell, John C. *Developing the Leader Within You*. Nashville, Tenn.: T. Nelson, 1993.

—. *The 21 Indispensable Qualities of a Leader: Becoming the Person that People Will Want to Follow*. Nashville, TN: T. Nelson, 1999.

McCalep, George O. *Sin in the House*. Lithonia: Orman Press, Inc., 1999.

—. *Stir Up the Gifts: Empowering Believers for Victorious Living and Ministry Tasks*. Lithonia, GA: Orman Press, 1999.

McEachern, Alton H. and Sunday School Board Southern Baptist Convention. *Proclaim the Gospel: A Guide to Biblical Preaching*. Nashville, TN: Convention Press, 1975.

Mosley, Ernest E. *Called to Joy: A Design for Pastoral Ministries*. Nashville, Tenn.: Convention Press, 1973.

Oswald, Roy M and Alban Institute. *The Pastor as Newcomer*. Washington, D.C.: Alban Institute, 1977.

Sanders, J. Oswald. *Spiritual Leadership*. 2nd Rev. Chicago: Moody Press, 1994.

Scott, Jr., Manuel. *Preacher, Wait Your Turn*. n.d.

Smith, Donald D. *Clergy in the Crossfire*. n.d.

Tidwell, Charles A. *Church Administration: Effective Leadership for Ministry*. Nashville, Tenn.: Broadman Press, 1985.

Towns, Elmer. *The 8 Laws of Leadership: Making Extraordinary Leaders out of Ordinary Believers*. Lynchburg, VA: Church Growth Institute, 1992.

*Webster's Encyclopedic Unabridged Dictionary of the English Language*. Avenel, N.J.: Grammercy Books, 1996.

www.ingramcontent.com/pod-product-compliance
Lightning Source LLC
Chambersburg PA
CBHW051901090426
42811CB00003B/421